Scott Foresman

Reading

Grade 6

Intervention Handbook

for Reading Success

Scott
Foresman

Editorial Offices: Glenview, Illinois • Parsippany, New Jersey • New York, New York
Sales Offices: Parsippany, New Jersey • Duluth, Georgia • Glenview, Illinois • Carrollton, Texas • Ontario, California

ISBN 0-328-02603-4

6 7 8 9 10 - V004 - 09 08 07 06 05 04

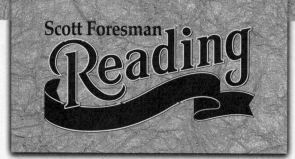

Scott Foresman

Reading

Intervention Handbook
for Reading Success

Contents
Section One

Section Two

© Scott Foresman 6

About Section One of This Handbook

This part of the *Scott Foresman Reading Intervention Handbook* is a collection of strategies and blackline masters designed for those students who need additional support to successfully work through a lesson in the *Scott Foresman Reading* program. The strategies provide specific routines to use before, during, and after reading. The chart on pages 5 and 6 describes behavior manifested by students having reading difficulties and recommends an appropriate strategy routine.

When using the strategy routines, you will notice references to graphic organizers. For your convenience reproducible blackline graphic organizers can be found on pages 22–33. An explanation of the graphic organizers is on page 7. The strategy routines also list specific *Scott Foresman Reading* products you can use for intervention. A description of these products can be found on pages 8 and 9. One of the products listed is Leveled Readers A and B. A listing of comprehension skills and corresponding Leveled Readers, Grades 1–6, can be found on page 96.

How to Use Section One of This Handbook

The strategy routines are designed to be used with certain sections of the *Scott Foresman Reading* Teacher's Editions —Skill Lessons, Activate Prior Knowledge, Vocabulary, Guiding Comprehension, Reader Response, Phonics, Word Study, and Fluency.

Use these suggestions as a guide to approaching the strategy routines.

- Use the chart on pages 5 and 6 as needed. The *If … then* statements detail the kinds of reading problems students may have and direct you to a specific strategy routine to use.

- Read over the strategy routine before using it. Note any products or materials you may want to use with the teaching of the strategy routine.

- Proceed step by step through the strategy routine with students.

- Use the Apply and Assess to check students' understanding and application of the routine.

- Repeat the routine as necessary.

"Teachers should . . . demonstrate how to apply each strategy successfully—what it is, how it is carried out, and when and why it should be used. Instead of just talking about a strategy, teachers need to illustrate the processes they use by thinking aloud, or modeling mental processes, while they read."

Linda G. Fielding and P. David Pearson,
"Reading Comprehension: What Works"

> *"... new information should be presented in a meaningful context and with substantial support from extra-linguistic cues such as visuals and demonstrations."*
>
> Anna Chamot,
> Michael O'Malley,
> "The Cognitive Academic Language Learning Approach"

> *"Making connections between images and definitions can help students remember word meanings."*
>
> Camille Blachowicz,
> Peter Fisher,
> *Teaching Vocabulary in all Classrooms*

> *"Children who are allowed to teach one another learn a valuable lesson in the process. They discover that people, even peers, can be good resources."*
>
> Donald Graves,
> Virginia Stuart,
> *Write from the Start*

What Good Readers Do	Intervention		Strategy Routine
Good readers organize their thoughts as they read a selection.	**If . . .** students have trouble keeping track of the people or events in a story or article,	**then . . .** have them use graphic organizers to record their ideas.	**Use Graphic Organizers, p. 10**
Good readers set purposes for listening to a selection read aloud.	**If . . .** students have difficulty focusing their attention while listening,	**then . . .** help them set a purpose and record it before listening to a selection.	**Set a Purpose for Listening, p. 11**
Good readers use visual cues to understand and clarify vocabulary and concepts.	**If . . .** students do not have a clear understanding of how demonstrations and illustrations can help them,	**then . . .** demonstrate how these visual cues can be used to explain concepts.	**Use Visual Cues, p. 11**
Good readers make text meaningful by relating it to something in their own lives.	**If . . .** students have difficulty making a connection between their own lives and the text,	**then . . .** guide them to use an audio to build background.	**Use Audio to Build Background, p. 12**
Good readers use visual cues to build understanding.	**If . . .** students are uncertain how to use visual cues,	**then . . .** help them use pictures and demonstrations in order to relate to the text.	**Use Visual Cues, p. 12**
Good readers associate new vocabulary words with things from their personal experience.	**If . . .** students have difficulty calling upon prior knowledge to help them learn and remember unfamiliar words,	**then . . .** have them record words and pictures on a Vocabulary Frame.	**Use Graphic Organizers, p. 13**
Good readers use prior knowledge when they preview and predict.	**If . . .** students are uncertain about how to preview a selection and make predictions about it,	**then . . .** model how to use the text, the pictures, and your own knowledge to preview and predict.	**Preview and Predict, p. 14**
Good readers set specific reading goals.	**If . . .** students have difficulty setting a reading purpose,	**then . . .** help them focus their attention on setting a single purpose.	**Set a Purpose for Reading, p. 14**
Good readers enjoy and benefit from reading with others.	**If . . .** students are hesitant to read with others,	**then . . .** provide guidelines for reading with one or more classmates.	**Read with a Partner or Group, p. 15**
Good readers can follow along as a selection is read aloud.	**If . . .** students have difficulty following a selection as it is being read aloud,	**then . . .** guide them through an oral reading of the selection.	**Read Along with an Oral Presentation, p. 15**

"The important thing about self-corrections is that children initiate them because they see that something is wrong and call up their own resources for working on a possible solution."

Billie J. Askew,
Irene C. Fountas,
"Building an Early
Reading Process:
Active from the Start!"

"When the reading is phrased like spoken language and the responding is fluent, then there is a fair chance that the reader can read for meaning and check what he reads against his language knowledge."

Marie M. Clay,
Reading Recovery

What Good Readers Do	Intervention		Strategy Routine
Good readers enhance their understanding and appreciation of text by relating it to their own personal experiences.	**If . . .** students have trouble connecting what they are reading with their own real-life experiences,	**then . . .** use a guiding comprehension question to model and explain how to relate text to personal experience.	**Relate Text to Personal Experience,** p. 16
Good readers know how to self-monitor and use fix-up strategies.	**If . . .** students are uncertain about when and how to help themselves when they are reading,	**then . . .** model how you monitor during reading by showing what you do when you don't understand something.	**Self-Monitor and Use Fix-Up Strategies,** p. 17
Good readers answer most questions about selections with confidence and success.	**If . . .** students have difficulty answering questions about selections,	**then . . .** present a routine for answering questions.	**Use a Routine to Answer Questions,** p. 18
Good readers know how to approach tests.	**If . . .** students have difficulty with test formats,	**then . . .** give them guidelines for taking tests.	**Use Test-taking Tips,** p. 18
Good readers can hear the sounds in words.	**If . . .** students have difficulty identifying the sounds that make up a word,	**then . . .** help them segment the word into its individual sounds and then blend those sounds to make the word.	**Use Blending and Segmenting,** p. 19
Good readers use decoding skills to figure out unfamiliar words.	**If . . .** students have trouble with letter-sound relationships,	**then . . .** demonstrate how word families can help students read and spell words.	**Use Word Families to Decode Text,** p. 19
Good readers understand how word parts combine and affect the meaning of a word.	**If . . .** students have difficulty recognizing and using word parts to figure out word meaning,	**then . . .** help students determine word meaning by identifying and defining the parts of the word.	**Use Word Parts to Understand Meaning,** p. 20
Good readers read fluently, decoding text automatically and focusing on meaning.	**If . . .** students read so slowly and laboriously, they cannot focus on meaning,	**then . . .** present a fluency routine they can practice using text that is familiar to them.	**Reread Familiar Text to Develop Fluency,** p. 21

About the Graphic Organizers

The following graphic organizers, found on pages 22–33, can be used with the strategy routines.

Vocabulary Frame is a creative way to get students to think about word meaning. Students activate prior knowledge by associating the word with something from personal experience. *Good for activating prior knowledge, predicting, and context clues.*

Story Prediction from Previewing calls upon students to use what they know as they preview the selection title and illustrations. Prediction activities motivate student interest, encourage readers to focus their attention, and give them a stake in the outcome of the story. *Good for predicting, activating prior knowledge, and drawing conclusions.*

Web 1 helps students highlight a central concept and connect it to related details. The web encourages students to generate ideas, recognize concept relationships, and organize information. *Good for main idea and supporting details and summarizing.*

Web 3 highlights a concept central to a selection or topic and allows students to relate and categorize details. Students who need help in connecting and organizing ideas will especially benefit from this organizer. *Good for main idea and supporting details and summarizing.*

K-W-L Chart helps students use what they know to generate interest in a selection. It encourages group members to share and discuss what they know, what they want to know, and what they learn about a topic. *Good for activating prior knowledge, setting purposes for reading, and summarizing.*

Plot/Story Sequence helps students recognize the sequence of events in a selection. Keeping track of the sequence of events is a simple way to give students a sense of story. Understanding sequence prepares students for more complex types of story structure. *Good for sequence, plot, recall and retell, text structure, and summarizing.*

Time Line helps students organize events from fiction and nonfiction in sequential order along a continuum. Not only do students see the events in order, but they are also exposed to the overall time frame in which the events occurred. *Good for sequence, summarizing, and text structure.*

Story Elements provides a framework for thinking that can help students write a summary of a story. It is particularly useful for students who need more guidance recognizing story structure and summarizing key events. *Good for character, setting, plot, theme, summarizing, sequence, and drawing conclusions.*

Cause and Effect helps students identify what happened and why it happened in both fiction and nonfiction. When students can see that there are causal relationships between events or ideas in text, they can make generalizations about other causal relationships in new texts and in life situations. *Good for cause and effect, summarizing, sequence, and text structure.*

Problem and Solution 1 helps students identify problems and solutions presented in fiction or nonfiction. It prompts students to recognize what is important in the story and how ideas or events are related to a problem. *Good for plot structure, summarizing, and text structure.*

T-Chart provides a visual framework to help students identify two items or concepts. Students can use the graphic organizer to chart ideas within a text, across texts, and between prior knowledge and new ideas. *Good for compare and contrast, main idea and supporting details, summarizing, and activating prior knowledge.*

Five-Column Chart provides a grid on which students can organize information for clearer understanding. It is a useful tool for exploring and classifying ideas, story elements, genres, or vocabulary features. *Good for compare and contrast, main idea and supporting details, summarizing, and activate prior knowledge.*

About *Scott Foresman Reading* Products

These Scott Foresman products are referenced within Section One of this handbook and are part of the *Scott Foresman Reading* program.

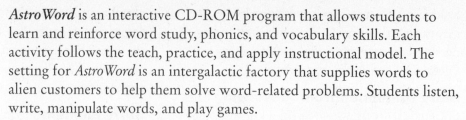

AstroWord is an interactive CD-ROM program that allows students to learn and reinforce word study, phonics, and vocabulary skills. Each activity follows the teach, practice, and apply instructional model. The setting for *AstroWord* is an intergalactic factory that supplies words to alien customers to help them solve word-related problems. Students listen, write, manipulate words, and play games.

Background Building Audio Cassette/CD helps students get ready to read the selection in the basal by building background and drawing upon their prior knowledge. Author interviews, radio broadcasts, historical recordings, and scene-setting sound effects encourage visualization and support concept development.

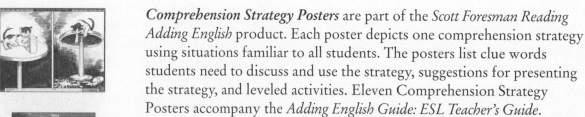

Comprehension Strategy Posters are part of the *Scott Foresman Reading Adding English* product. Each poster depicts one comprehension strategy using situations familiar to all students. The posters list clue words students need to discuss and use the strategy, suggestions for presenting the strategy, and leveled activities. Eleven Comprehension Strategy Posters accompany the *Adding English Guide: ESL Teacher's Guide*.

Daily Word Routines Flip Chart provides quick activities for students to practice phonics, word study, vocabulary, and language.

Grade 3 *Phonemic Awareness and Phonics Manipulatives Kit* helps students practice phonics and word-building through hands-on activities and multi-sensory games.

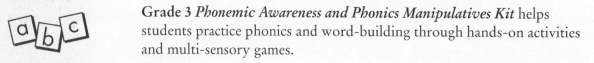

Grade 3 *Phonics Sourcebook* provides blackline masters of words and letter manipulatives and games from the *Phonemic Awareness and Phonics Manipulatives Kit*. If the kit is not accessible, the sourcebook can be used in its place.

Graphic Organizer Transparencies help students build comprehension, learn how to organize information, and model higher-thinking skills. They may be used to model how students complete their own graphic organizer.

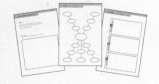

Leveled Readers A and B are for those students needing a lower-level reading selection. They are written one to one and a half grades below grade level. For every main selection in the basal Student Edition, there is a corresponding Set A Leveled Reader (Easy) and a Set B Leveled Reader (Easy/Average). The books reinforce each lesson's target comprehension skill and provide practice with the selection vocabulary. See page 96 for an overview of *Scott Foresman Reading A* and *B Leveled Readers* in Grades 1–6. For your convenience, the Leveled Readers are listed according to the comprehension skills they cover.

Leveled Reader Resource Guide includes instructional plans and practice for each Leveled Reader. The guide provides strategies for guided reading, vocabulary development, and on-going assessment.

Scott Foresman Know Zone™ website helps students prepare for tests by providing test-preparation techniques, practice, and reinforcement. Log on to the Know Zone™ at www.kz.com or connect to it through the *Scott Foresman Reading Headquarters Website.*

Scott Foresman Reading Headquarters Website, at www.sfreading.com, offers Internet Workshops that extend the Student Edition selections by having students investigate a topic on the Internet, then write ideas, and share them with their class.

Selection Audio Cassette/CD includes recordings of all Student Edition selections in the basal. The selections are recorded to allow students, especially those working below level, to follow along as the selection is read aloud.

Ten Important Sentences is a booklet that provides the ten most important sentences for every main selection in the basal Student Edition. Each sentence in the booklet includes a key idea from the selection to help build the skills students need for comprehension. Blackline masters, strategies, and activities for using the sentences are included in the booklet.

TestWorks for Scott Foresman Reading is a CD-ROM that allows teachers to customize multiple-choice tests, free-response tests, and practice tests for students.

© Scott Foresman 6

Strategy Routines for Skill Lessons

Use Graphic Organizers

About the Strategy

Mapping out a concept can help students understand what they read. Graphic organizers can help students improve reading comprehension skills as they move from mere memorization tasks to real learning experiences.

How to Use the Strategy

1 **Introduce** the idea of a graphic organizer to students. Explain that it will help them organize their thoughts as they work through a reading selection.

2 **Select** a graphic organizer appropriate for the skill lesson selection students are currently reading.

3 **Display** the graphic organizer as an overhead transparency or as a blackline master.

4 **Read** through the graphic organizer with students. Always partially complete the graphic organizer with them. This will help students focus and understand what they are doing and why.

Apply and Assess

Students can work independently, in pairs, or in small groups to complete the graphic organizer. Bring the group back together to discuss the information they recorded and how the organizer helped.

The following is a list of graphic organizers you can use with skill lessons. See page 7 for a description of each organizer and the skills it can support. Graphic organizers in blackline master form can be found on pages 22–33.

If available, you may want to use the *Graphic Organizer Transparencies.*

Set a Purpose for Listening

About the Strategy

Setting a purpose for listening helps students focus attention while listening.

How to Use the Strategy

1. **Introduce** the skill lesson selection by going over the title, author, and any llustrations. Ask students what they would like to find out or set a purpose for students.

2. **Work** with students to write a statement or question that reflects the purpose. For example: Listen to find what Meg likes and dislikes about baseball.

3. **Discuss** the selection after students have listened to it. Refer back to the sentence to keep students focused. Use a graphic organizer, such as the T-Chart, to keep track of the discussion.

Apply and Assess

Students can write a brief paragraph or make an illustration to demonstrate an understanding of the purpose they listened for.

If available, you may want students to listen to the skill selection read aloud on the *Selection Audio.*

Selection Audio

Use Visual Cues

About the Strategy

Visual cues such as pictures or demonstrations may help students understand vocabulary and concepts, such as cause-cffect relationships.

How to Use the Strategy

1. **Show** a picture or demonstrate the skill with props. For example, for the skill of cause and effect, show a picture of a shattered glass. (Always choose pictures that will be familiar to your students.)

2. **Describe** or have students describe the picture.

3. **Ask** students literal and inferential questions about what they see. Phrase questions so that students focus on the skill. For the picture of the shattered glass ask students what they see. Ask what might be a reason (cause) that the glass shattered (effect).

Cause	Effect

4. **Record** students' responses on the Cause and Effect or T-Chart graphic organizer.

Apply and Assess

Present a new visual cue for the skill or for a different skill. Students can work in pairs or small groups to complete a graphic organizer for the skill. Have students share completed organizers with the group, telling what visual cues helped them.

If available, you may want to use *Comprehension Strategy Posters* from *Adding English* for teaching a comprehension skill using visual cues.

Strategy Routines for Activate Prior Knowledge

Use Audio to Build Background

About the Strategy

To hear a cow mooing or the sound of a train whistle can help students relate a selection to their own lives. Building background through audio can help students make reading the text more meaningful.

How to Use the Strategy

1 **Introduce** the contents of the CD/tape. If students will be listening to a speaker, sound effects, or a song, discuss it first. Guide students in setting a purpose for listening. Have students write it down.

2 **Discuss** the contents of the CD/tape after students have listened.

3 **Record** on the board or graphic organizer students' thoughts.

4 **Replay** the tape as needed for further discussion or for clarification.

Apply and Assess

Students can work together or individually to complete a graphic organizer about the recording. Bring the group back together to discuss what they wrote and what they learned from the audio.

If available, you may want students to listen to the *Background-Building Audio.*

Background-Building Audio

Use Visual Cues

About the Strategy

Visual representations engage students before they read. Visual cues such as pictures, demonstrations, or dramatizations help build understanding.

How to Use the Strategy

1 **Show** a picture or do a demonstration of something related to the selection students will be reading. For example, if the story is about baseball, use a ball and a bat to introduce the selection.

2 **Help** students relate the visual cue to something in their own lives.

3 **Use** graphic organizers, such as the T-Chart or Five-Column Chart, to capture students' ideas and thoughts related to the selection.

Apply and Assess

Using the graphic organizer, students can work individually or in pairs to write a list of items that they think will relate to the selection. Have students tell what the item is and how it relates.

If you have access to the *Scott Foresman Reading Headquarters Website*, you may want to visit the Internet Workshop section at www.sfreading.com to expand upon ideas in the selections students will be reading.

Strategy Routine for Vocabulary

Use Graphic Organizers

About the Strategy

Using graphic organizers, such as a Vocabulary Frame, can help students think about word meaning by associating words with something from personal experiences. Calling upon prior knowledge can help students predict, learn, and retain the meanings of unfamiliar words.

How to Use the Strategy

1 **Limit** the number of new words students need to know. Share the words and discuss their meanings with students.

2 **Work** through the Vocabulary Frame graphic organizer on page 22 with students. Students can have their own copy of the organizer, writing along with you. Write a vocabulary word, such as *instruments*, in the word box. Ask students to suggest a picture or symbol they think might help them remember the meaning of the word. Then draw the image in the association box. Students should put this same information on their organizers.

3 **Ask** a volunteer to suggest a definition for the word and then give a sentence using it. Write the definition and sentence on the organizer. Students should write this definition and sentence on their copies.

4 **Verify** the definition by having students use a dictionary or glossary to find the word. Write this definition on the appropriate lines and have students do the same.

5 **Have** students provide a second example sentence based on the verified definition and write this sentence on their organizers.

6 **Repeat** as necessary using other words.

Apply and Assess

Students can work individually or in pairs to complete Vocabulary Frames for other new words they are learning. Bring the group back together and have them share their organizers for each of the words.

Other graphic organizers that can be used for vocabulary include the following: Web 1, p. 24; Web 3, p. 25; T-Chart, p. 32; Five-Column Chart, p. 33.

If available, you may want to use any or all of these products for more vocabulary practice: the *Graphic Organizer Transparencies* and the *Daily Word Routines Flip Chart*.

Strategy Routines for Reading Strategies

Preview and Predict

About the Strategy

By previewing a selection, students can draw upon what they already know to understand what they are about to read. Previewing helps students formulate predictions based on prior knowledge.

How to Use the Strategy

1 **Read** aloud or have a student read the title, author, and a paragraph or two. Have students look at any illustrations or photographs.

2 **Model** using the text and pictures to predict what a selection will be about. For example, for the story "Addie in Charge," say, "The head-note tells that Addie has been left in charge of the farm. I know that pioneer children know a lot about farming. The pictures show that Addie faces a fire. I predict that Addie will not save the farm but will save herself and her brother."

3 **Write** your prediction on the board. Have students work individually, in pairs, or small groups to write their predictions.

Apply and Assess

Bring the group back together to compare and explain their predictions.

If available, use *Leveled Readers A* or *B* for lower-leveled selections to preview and predict.

Set a Purpose for Reading

About the Strategy

Setting a purpose before reading helps students establish a clear focus and enables them to direct their attention to a specific reading goal.

How to Use the Strategy

1 **Preview** the selection by reading the title, author, introductory notes, if they exist, and/or a paragraph or two.

2 **Ask** students what they hope to find out when they read the selection. Write their responses on the board.

3 **Use** the list on the board to set a single purpose with students for reading. Discard all other responses.

4 **Begin** a graphic organizer such as a K-W-L chart with students to help them organize their thoughts.

K What I Know	W What I Want to Know	L What I Learned

Apply and Assess

As they read, students can work individually or in pairs to complete the graphic organizer. Bring the group together to discuss the organizer.

If available, use *Leveled Readers A* or *B* for lower-leveled selections to set a purpose for reading and the *Graphic Organizer Transparencies*.

Read with a Partner or Group

About the Strategy

As students read with a partner or group, they increase comprehension and confidence to read better as they interact and discuss what was read.

How to Use the Strategy

1 **Choose** for students a partner or small group to read the selection with. If pairing, pair a less fluent reader with a more fluent reader.

2 **Write** the following partner reading cues on a chart or the board.
   a. Decide who will read first.
   b. Decide where to stop and switch readers.
   c. Stop and discuss sections you don't understand.
   d. After reading, talk about what you have read.

3 **Monitor** the reading from a distance and check progress after students have finished.

Apply and Assess

Students can track their reading by using a graphic organizer such as Problem and Solution 1 or by taking notes and writing a brief summary. Let students share their notes with the group.

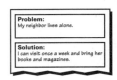

Problem:
My neighbor lives alone.

Solution:
I can visit once a week and bring her books and magazines.

If available, use *Leveled Readers A* or *B* for lower-level selections to read and the *Graphic Organizer Transparencies*.

Read Along with an Oral Presentation

About the Strategy

Hearing a selection read aloud can make the text come alive for students. When students read along as a selection is being read aloud, they often gain confidence to read it by themselves.

How to Use the Strategy

1 **Decide** who will read the selection aloud. Will you read it aloud, will an audio version be played, or will students take turns reading?

2 **Set** guidelines for readers to follow, such as stopping at certain points, reading with expression, or changing voices to suit the material.

3 **Have** students follow along as the selection is read aloud. You may want to stop at predetermined spots for clarification or questions.

4 **Work** with students to summarize the most important ideas.

Apply and Assess

Students can use a graphic organizer, such as Plot/Story Sequence, to summarize what they have learned as they listened to the story being read.

If available, you may want to use any or all of the following products: the *Selection Audio* for students to hear the selection read aloud, *Ten Important Sentences* to help students summarize, and the *Graphic Organizer Transparencies*.

Selection Audio

© Scott Foresman 6

Strategy Routines for Guiding Comprehension

Relate Text to Personal Experience

About the Strategy

Relating text to students' life experiences helps students become more involved with what they read and increases their comprehension, appreciation, and motivation to read.

How to Use the Strategy

1 **Choose** one of the guiding comprehension questions in the *Scott Foresman Reading* Teacher's Edition. Write it on the board or use a graphic organizer such as Web 1 or Problem and Solution 1.

2 **Model** how you would answer the question. For example: *Question:* Why do you think Marianne touches the feather in her pocket as she says, "She'll be there. She'll want me." *Answer:* I think Marianne is hoping to find her real mother. I think Marianne is touching the feather for good luck. By touching the feather, it makes her feel calm and assured that her mother just might be there.

3 **Relate** your answer to a personal, real-life situation or make a cross-content connection. For example, you might say, "Sometimes when I watch my daughter play a basketball game, I cross my fingers when she takes a shot. I know that her talent and practice will help her make the shot, but I still cross my fingers for luck. I think Marianne is touching the feather for the same reason. What do you think?" Allow students time to offer their opinions.

4 **Guide** students through another question in a similar manner. Have students relate their answers to a personal, real-life situation.

Apply and Assess

Have students work in pairs or small groups to answer one or two of the guided reading questions about the selection. Questions can be written on the board or on a graphic organizer. The group can come back together and share their answers.

If available, you may want to use the *Leveled Readers A* or *B* for lower-level selections and the accompanying *Leveled Reader Resource Guide* which contains guiding comprehension questions.

Self-Monitor and Use Fix-Up Strategies

About the Strategy

Learning when, where, and how to self-monitor and use fix-up strategies can help students check their reading comprehension, enabling them to become independent, fluent readers.

How to Use the Strategy

1. **Demonstrate** what you do when you are reading and don't understand something. Explain that you stop reading and try to identify what is causing the confusion. For example, say: "I've read a few pages, and a lot has happened already. I understood everything until this last part—it doesn't make sense to me. I think I should stop reading and ask myself: What things have happened so far in this story? Did I miss something that's important? What should I do now?"

2. **Model** using an appropriate fix-up strategy. For example, for the strategy of reread and review, say: "I will read this page again. I am not sure why Laura was afraid of the badger. I will read the page again more slowly to see if there's something I missed."

3. **Focus** on only one fix-up strategy at a time, such as reread and review. Students should practice one fix-up strategy over a period of time until they are able to do the strategy themselves without prompting or help.

4. **Use** a graphic organizer so students can organize their thoughts. You may want to continue the graphic organizer students began in Activate Prior Knowledge or begin a new graphic organizer such as a K-W-L chart or a graphic organizer that better fits a particular skill such as sequence.

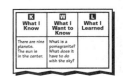

The following are some fix-up strategies you may want to use with students.

adjust reading rate

read on

reread and review

seek help from others

seek help from reference sources

skim and scan

use text features

write notes

Apply and Assess

Have students work in pairs to complete a graphic organizer together. Have them record the fix-up strategy they use on the organizer. Remind partners to stop reading when one of them doesn't understand something and to use the fix-up strategy. Bring the group back together after reading. Have pairs summarize what they have read and how the fix-up strategy helped them.

If available, you may want to use the *Graphic Organizer Transparencies*.

Strategy Routines for Reader Response

Use a Routine to Answer Questions

About the Strategy

When given a routine to answer questions about a selection, students can answer the questions with confidence and success.

How to Use the Strategy

 Discuss the following routine with students.
   a. *Read each question carefully.* This can help students decide what information is being asked for.
   b. *Put the question in your own words.* This can help students figure out what a question means or what information is needed.
   c. *Reread the text.* This can help clarify meaning or explain an answer.

2 **Work** through a question with students using the routine and a Five-Column Chart graphic organizer.

Apply and Assess

Students can work in small groups to answer each remaining question using the Five-Column Chart graphic organizer. Groups can share and discuss their responses.

If available, you may want to use the *Graphic Organizer Transparencies.*

Use Test-taking Tips

About the Strategy

When students understand how to take a test, they perform better and become more confident in their answers.

How to Use the Strategy

 Write the following test-taking tips on a chart or the board.
   a. Read all the directions carefully before you begin.
   b. Read the entire question and all the choices before trying to answer multiple-choice questions.
   c. Look for key words that signal what is needed for the answer.
   d. Skim the selection to find related phrases or sentences that might contain the answer.
   e. Eliminate answer choices that are clearly incorrect in multiple-choice questions.

2 **Demonstrate** each tip, using a test students have already taken.

Apply and Assess

Have students complete a practice test. Upon completion of the test, have them explain what test-taking tips they used and how the tips helped.

If available, you may want to log on to the *Know Zone*™ at www.kz.com or connect to it through the *Scott Foresman Reading Headquarters Website* at www.sfreading.com to do a practice test. You can customize tests for students using *TestWorks for Scott Foresman Reading.*

© Scott Foresman 6

Strategy Routines for Phonics

Use Blending and Segmenting

About the Strategy

Blending and segmenting is a crucial phonemic awareness skill students need to develop for decoding and syllabication. When they can hear the sounds in words, they can associate those sounds with letters.

How to Use the Strategy

1. **Say** a vocabulary, spelling, or one-syllable word such as *tops* slowly. Have students repeat it. Ask how many sounds they hear. (4)

2. **Segment** the sounds in the word, saying each sound /t/ /o/ /p/ /s/. Have students say the sounds after you.

3. **Blend** the sounds together. Have students blend the sounds together to say the word: *tops.* Tell them to listen for all four sounds.

Apply and Assess

Present pictures of one-syllable words such as a cat and a coat. Working with one word at a time, say each sound in the word. Have students blend the sounds to say the word and point to the picture being named.

If available, you may want to use the Grade 3 *Phonics Sourcebook* or the Grade 3 *Phonemic Awareness and Phonics Manipulatives Kit* for visual or kinesthetic learners.

Use Word Families to Decode Text

About the Strategy

Using word families can help strengthen students' decoding skills as they recognize the relationship between words that sound the same.

How to Use the Strategy

1. **Write** on the board and say a word that students know, such as *round*.

2. **Ask** students to name other words that rhyme with *round*. Write students' responses on the board.

3. **Circle** the similar part of each word, such as the *ound* in *round*. Help students recognize that only the initial letter or letters change, and if they can read and spell a word such as *round*, then they can read and spell other words with a similar sound.

4. **Repeat** as necessary with other words.

Apply and Assess

Have students work in pairs or teams to make word families from ending sounds, such as *ate, ight, ash,* and *oon*. Students can share their words.

If available, you may want to use the Grade 3 *Phonics Sourcebook* or the Grade 3 *Phonemic Awareness and Phonics Manipulatives Kit.*

Strategy Routine for Word Study

Use Word Parts to Understand Meaning

About the Strategy

Recognizing word parts and understanding how they combine and contribute to the meaning of a word, can help students determine the meanings of unfamiliar words.

How to Use the Strategy

1 **Write** on the board a sentence containing a compound word or a word with an affix or ending. Examples: *The children dislike that game. Where is the cookbook? The puppy is playful.* Have students read the sentence.

2 **Circle** the word you want students to focus on, for example, *dislike, cookbook,* or *playful.* Discuss its meaning.

3 **Write** the word again and underline the affix, ending, or two words that make up the compound word.

4 **Explain** or let volunteers explain the meaning of any word part and how it affects the meaning of the word. For example: When *dis-* is added to the word *like,* it makes the word mean the opposite. *Dislike* means "to not like."

5 **Ask** students to think of other words for the word part being discussed. For example, for *dis-* students might suggest: *disagree, disappear, disable,* and *disconnect.*

Apply and Assess

Students can work independently, in pairs, or in groups. Present sentences from text students are reading that contain compound words or words with affixes or endings. Have students write the word, its base word, the word part, and tell what the word means. Bring the group back together to share their findings.

If available, you may want to use any or all of these products for more word-study practice: the Grade 3 *Phonics Sourcebook,* Grade 3 *Phonemic Awareness and Phonics Manipulatives Kit, AstroWord* (Discs B and C), *Daily Word Routines Flip Chart.*

Strategy Routine for Fluency

Reread Familiar Text to Develop Fluency

About the Strategy

Fluent readers are able to decode text automatically, and as a result they can focus on meaning, develop greater confidence, and enjoy reading more.

How to Use the Strategy

1 Write on the board or on an overhead the following routine. Have students copy it to refer to later.
   a. Preview your reading and decide how to pronounce proper nouns.
   b. Practice reading difficult words so you read them more smoothly.
   c. Check pronunciations in a dictionary.
   d. Use punctuation correctly. Pause at commas. Let your voice rise and fall with end punctuation.
   e. Match your tone of voice to the tone of the piece.
   f. Use appropriate phrasing to build excitement or add emphasis.

2 Help students select a passage from a familiar story.

3 Model reading the passage aloud showing how a fluent reader sounds.

4 Discuss each point with students and demonstrate how to follow the routine.

Apply and Assess

Allow time for students to practice reading. Direct them to read the passage several times as they focus on the routine. Listen to students read aloud. Students can read to a partner or a small group. Allow students to use the fluency routine to critique each other on how well the selection was read.

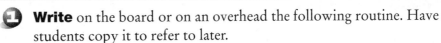

If available, you may want to use *Leveled Readers A* or *B* for a fluency check.

Word

Association or Symbol

Predicted definition: _____

One good sentence:

_____

_____

_____

_____

Verified definition:

_____

_____

_____

Another good sentence:

_____

_____

_____

_____

Title _____

Read the title and look at the pictures in the story.
What do you think a problem in the story might be?

I think a problem might be _____

_____

_____

After reading _____,
draw a picture of one of the problems in the story.

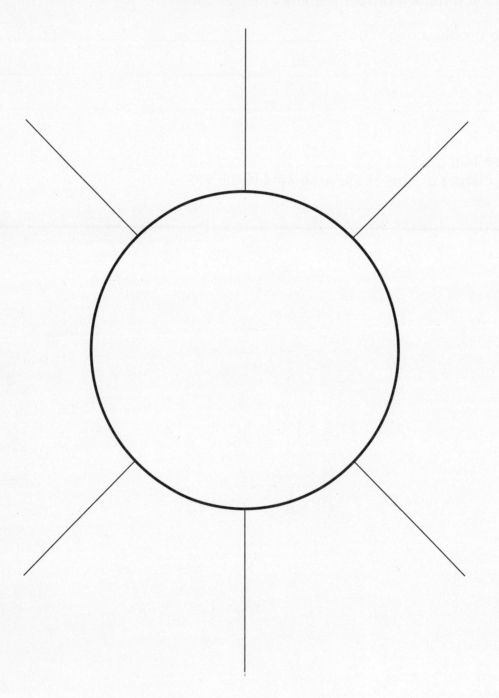

Topic

What We **K** now	What We **W** ant to Know	What We **L** earned

Title _____

Beginning

Middle

End

Date _____

Title _____

This story is about _____

_____
(name the characters)

This story takes place _____

_____
(where and when)

The action begins when _____

_____

_____

Then, _____

_____

Next, _____

_____

After that, _____

_____

The story ends when _____

_____

_____

Theme: _____

Cause   **Effect**

Why did it happen?	**What happened?**

Why did it happen?	**What happened?**

Why did it happen?	**What happened?**

Problem

Solution

About Section Two of This Handbook

This section of the *Scott Foresman Reading Intervention Handbook* contains text and instruction designed to provide extra support for the struggling reader. It is important for all students to experience successful and meaningful reading. Providing students with reading materials that are at an appropriate instructional level and that students *want* to read is the first step toward developing fluent readers.

Students who are not able to read the main selections in the Student Edition will be able to read the Selection Summaries included in this handbook. The summaries will allow struggling students to participate in the same discussions and instruction as their classmates.

This section of the handbook also includes easy-to-follow teaching notes for the Selection Summaries and for the stories in *Collection for Readers*. These lessons provide the kinds of predictable routines that struggling readers need and that make learning possible.

You may want to follow the plan below with students who cannot read the main selection and who will read the Selection Summaries and the stories in *Collection for Readers* instead. (See the weekly 5-Day Planner in the Teacher's Edition for selection-specific information.)

Day 1 Include students in the Skill Lesson, Activate Prior Knowledge, and Introduce Vocabulary with the rest of the class.

Day 2 Have students read the selection summary and answer the "What Do You Think?" questions while their classmates read the main selection.

Day 3 Let students listen to the main selection on audiotape while their classmates finish the main selection. For additional instruction on the target comprehension skill introduced in the Skill Lesson on Day 1, students should listen to the Reteach Lesson following the main selection on the audiotape. Include students in Reader Response about the main selection.

Day 4 / 5 Have students read and discuss the related selection from *Collection for Readers*.

© Scott Foresman 6

Selection Summaries

Selection Summaries for every main selection in the Student Edition are included to provide scaffolding for students reading significantly below grade level. Selection summaries are written for students who are reading so far below grade level that they cannot read the main selection. The summaries allow students to be part of class discussions and instruction whenever possible.

Selection Summaries

- focus on story concepts that are central to meaning.

- retell, or summarize, the main selection in the core program.

- include related vocabulary and tested vocabulary words from the main selection, when appropriate.

- provide three response questions that focus on critical thinking, vocabulary, and making connections to the main selection.

- begin with a motivating question to invite students to read further.

- are provided in this handbook in blackline master form.

Collection for Readers

Collection for Readers is an anthology of selections designed to provide additional alternate text for students reading significantly below grade level. These very easy leveled readers are written two grades below grade level. Research shows that struggling readers need to read more, but unfortunately, they often end up reading less. *Collection for Readers* provides a mix of fiction and nonfiction text and is designed to be appealing to students.

The selections in *Collection for Readers*

- **are written two grade levels below** each main selection and increase in difficulty to parallel the main selections in the Student Edition.

- **support vocabulary development** through systematic repetition of high-frequency words and introduction of selection vocabulary.

- **enhance comprehension** of each selection with three response questions in *Collection for Readers.*
  Question 1 provides a graphic organizer for the purpose of understanding text/story structure.
  Question 2 practices 1 of 5 identified comprehension skills.
  Question 3 practices critical thinking skills.

- **are a source for Guided Reading.**

- **provide high-interest text that is thematically-related or topically-related to the main selections** in the Student Edition.

Lesson plans for teaching the selections in the *Collection for Readers* are available in this handbook: for fiction, see pages 76-77; for nonfiction, see pages 78-79. Also see pages 86–93 of this handbook for a list of the vocabulary words, high-frequency words, and comprehension skills practiced in *Collection for Readers* for this grade.

The *Collection for Readers* is also available in a Take-Home version. These blackline masters allow students to practice reading each selection as an individual reader at home. The Take-Home version also has blackline masters of the key graphic organizers that accompany the selections.

Skills in Collection for Readers

Text/Story Structure

Question 1 after every selection in *Collection for Readers* provides a **graphic organizer in the student book.** Students can copy the graphic organizer onto a piece of paper, or you can provide them with a blackline master, available in the *Collection for Readers* Take-Home version. Question 1 offers these students the opportunity to routinely practice identifying the text or story structure before they answer other comprehension questions. These structures include:

- cause and effect

- compare and contrast

- main idea and supporting details

- plot/sequence of events

- problem/solution

Comprehension Skills

Support for comprehension skill instruction is provided with the graphic organizers found in the Take-Home version of the *Collection for Readers* and the lesson plans for *Collection for Readers*, pages 76-79. After every selection in *Collection for Readers*. Question 2 will ask students to practice one of five key comprehension skills. These are the key skills that students frequently struggle with on state and national standardized tests.

These key comprehension skills are

- main idea and details

- sequence

- drawing conclusions

- cause and effect

- compare and contrast

What Are Selection Summaries?

As part of its Intervention Handbook, *Scott Foresman Reading* provides summaries of each main selection from the Student Edition. The Selection Summaries provide text for students who are reading significantly below level and are unable to read the main selection. The goal of the Selection Summaries is to provide extra support so that struggling readers are better prepared to join on-level readers in group discussions and response activities pertaining to the main selection.

How Do the Summaries Assist Struggling Readers?

Because the summaries are written below grade level, they are more accessible to struggling readers. These simple retellings of the main selection from the Student Edition help students succeed in the core reading program by focusing on story concepts and vocabulary at the struggling reader's level.

The easy readability of the summaries makes it possible for students to engage in routine rereading, which is key to reading success. Because the number of words students read is critical to developing fluency, it is vital that struggling readers read more, not less. For this reason, rereading should be emphasized.

Teaching Notes

Activate Prior Knowledge Include struggling readers when you activate prior knowledge and introduce vocabulary prior to the main selection in the Student Edition. If appropriate, you may want to include struggling readers when you teach the Skill Lesson in the Student Edition as well. Whenever possible it is important to include struggling readers in the instruction their classmates receive.

Motivate and Read To spark students' interest, each summary begins with a motivating question that is tied to the selection concepts. Use the motivating question to introduce the summary and to help students set purposes for reading. Ask them if the motivating question makes them curious about what they are about to read. Ask if there are any questions they want to add before they begin reading. Students can write their questions.

Give students an opportunity to make connections to the concepts introduced during background-building with the class. Have students make predictions about the selection. Question what they think the story will be about. Then have students read the Selection Summary while classmates read the main selection.

© Scott Foresman 6

Concept Development Each summary also includes three questions in "What Do You Think?" The first question asks students to think about what they've read and to draw upon their own experiences to help them develop an understanding of important selection concepts. Talking with students about the meaning of the text helps them develop strategies they can use when they read and respond to other selections. Struggling readers must be given the opportunity to talk about what they read—before, during, and after reading. Book talk is an important step in helping the student develop into a confident reader. Therefore, these questions sometimes prompt students to share their thoughts and ideas with friends or family members.

Vocabulary The second question focuses on vocabulary development. In all cases, the vocabulary words included here are central to the understanding of the summary. Tested vocabulary words from the main selection are used in the summaries so that students can develop vocabulary knowledge using the same words as their classmates.

Sometimes the vocabulary question asks the reader to find a particular word in the summary based on a simple definition. Then students are asked to relate the word to their own knowledge, ideas, or experiences and create an illustration that shows their understanding of the word. Other times the vocabulary question asks readers to retell what they've read using specific words from the summary. Occasionally they are asked to illustrate an important scene from the retelling.

Connect to the Main Selection Once students have read the summary, they should listen to the selection audio (if available) and follow along in the Student Edition. The final "What Do You Think?" question is intended to help readers think beyond the summary and make connections to the main selection based on their listening. If students were included in the instruction for the Skill Lesson with classmates, you may want to have them listen to the Reteach Lesson following the main selection on the audiotape to apply the same target comprehension skill. An answer key for all "What Do You Think?" questions can be found on pages 70-75 of this book.

Students who have read the selection summary (and listened to the main selection on audiotape) should participate in Reader Response following classmates' completion of the main selection.

*Read about a boy who learns to sail.
What kind of adventures will he have?*

Tony and the Snark

Tony, age 11, saved $300 to buy a motorbike. But his father said Tony was not old enough to drive a motorbike. Instead, Tony bought a small sailboat named the *Snark*.

Tony did not want to spend part of the summer at his grandmother's house. She lived in a small town by the ocean in Connecticut, and Tony did not know anyone there. He and his parents tied the *Snark* to the top of their car for the trip.

When Tony arrived, Grandma Souza had a surprise. Tony would be taking sailing lessons from Chris Carluci. Tony was surprised when Chris turned out to be a teenage girl.

Chris taught Tony sailing words like *port, tiller,* and *luff. Port* is the left side of the boat when you are facing the bow. *Tiller* is the stick attached to the rudder, and *luff* is to turn into the wind. Then they put the *Snark* into the water. Chris showed Tony how to turn and stop the *Snark*. She sailed the boat around the cove. Then she said it was Tony's turn. Chris told him to sail around Horse Island. The *Snark* was moving very fast. Tony was filled with excitement. He was sailing! Suddenly Chris warned Tony that they were too close to the rocky island. He jerked the tiller to avoid submerged rocks. The boat capsized.

To Tony's surprise, the water was only four feet deep. Chris pointed out that it was good that they capsized because Tony learned what it was like. It's not too scary. She said Tony would make a terrific sailor. Tony realized he would enjoy his summer after all.

What Do You Think?

1. Think about the events in the story. Explain the things that did not happen the way Tony expected.

2. Find the word that means "covered by water." Have you ever seen something covered by water? Explain why this could be dangerous if you were sailing a boat.

3. Did you listen to the story on tape? If so, how would you describe the town of Swallows Bay? Would you like to live there? Why or why not?

Have you ever heard of Jackie Robinson?
Read about how he broke baseball's color barrier.

Teammates

In the 1940s all Major League baseball players were white. Branch Rickey was the general manager of the Brooklyn Dodgers. He wanted to change things. He thought his team should have the best players he could find. He felt everyone should have a chance to compete on ball fields across America. Branch Rickey searched the Negro Leagues for a good baseball player who would be right for the job. He chose Jackie Robinson.

Jackie Robinson became a hero to black people. They knew if he succeeded, others would follow. But Robinson did not have an easy time with the Dodgers. He faced much racial prejudice, including threats on his life. Some of his own teammates would not sit at the same table with him. But Robinson did not give up. Over time, his teammates began to respect his talent and his courage.

Pee Wee Reese was one of Robinson's teammates. Reese had grown up in Kentucky. He had rarely seen a black person. Most of his friends and relatives hated the idea that he was playing on the same team as a black man. During a game in Cincinnati, fans yelled hateful things when Robinson was on the field. Reese walked over and put his arm around Robinson's shoulders. The crowd became silent. In this way Pee Wee Reese showed that he supported his teammate, Jackie Robinson.

What Do You Think?

1. How do you think the author feels about Jackie Robinson? What makes you think so?

2. Retell the selection using the words below. Make an illustration of the most important scene from your retelling of the story.

    racial   **prejudice**   **hateful**

3. Did you listen to the selection on tape? If so, what can you add about Pee Wee Reese?

© Scott Foresman 6

Have you ever been embarrassed by your parents?
Find out how April Ellis solves this "muddy" problem.

April's Mud

April Ellis was glad no one at her school knew where she lived. The Ellis family lived in a school bus painted with bright colors. April's parents planned to build a house out of *adobe,* or dried mud.

April and her brother called their parents Tom and Susan. April's grandparents said Tom and Susan were hippies. Tom wore overalls and a ponytail. Susan wore bright clothes and silver jewelry. They grew most of their own food.

A neighbor, Mr. Flores, gave the Ellises good advice about building an adobe house. They mixed dirt and water to make mud. They poured the mud into wooden forms to make bricks. Tom insisted on making their adobe home in the traditional way. When April saw the floor plan for the house, she realized that it would have one big room and a dirt floor. She wanted a house with her own bedroom like her friends at school had. Why couldn't her parents be normal?

One day April's teacher, Mr. Wilder, said April's father had offered to help the class build an *horno,* or adobe oven. April worried about what her friends would think of Tom. But as her father worked with the class, April felt proud. The other kids really liked her father. They thought making the adobe bricks was fun. She realized that having a different kind of house might not be so bad after all.

What Do You Think?

1. Sometimes things don't turn out the way we expect. What caused April to feel proud of her family?

2. Retell the story using the words below. Make an illustration of what you think the adobe house will look like.

   adobe   **normal**   **traditional**

3. Did you listen to the story on tape? If so, what else did you learn about April's feelings? How would you have felt in her place?

© Scott Foresman 6

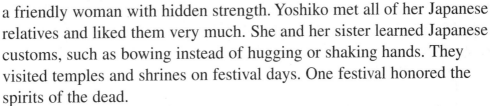

*What if you felt out of place no matter where you were?
Read about how a girl learns to feel good about herself.*

Hot Dogs and Bamboo Shoots

Yoshiko Uchida had two grandmothers. One lived in California, like Yoshiko. The other grandmother lived in Japan. Yoshiko's family often visited her grandmother, called Obah San, in Los Angeles. Each year on New Year's Day the whole family gathered at Obah San's house. They ate traditional Japanese foods. Yoshiko and her sister learned American songs and dances from their older cousins.

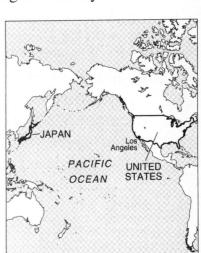

When Yoshiko was 12 years old, her parents decided to travel to Japan for the first time in ten years. Obah San went with them. After the ship left the harbor, Yoshiko felt seasick for four days. When she felt better, she enjoyed the trip.

When they arrived in Japan, Yoshiko's mother was very happy to see her own mother after so many years. Grandmother Umegaki was a friendly woman with hidden strength. Yoshiko met all of her Japanese relatives and liked them very much. She and her sister learned Japanese customs, such as bowing instead of hugging or shaking hands. They visited temples and shrines on festival days. One festival honored the spirits of the dead.

In Japan, Yoshiko looked like everyone else but she felt out of place because she couldn't read Japanese. Yoshiko knew she was really an American inside. But she realized she was not all American or all Japanese. She was a mixture of the two cultures, and that was a good thing.

What Do You Think?

1. What lesson did Yoshiko learn? How did she learn it?

2. Find the word that means "handed down from one generation to the next." Does your family have any foods that have been handed down? Explain. Tell how to make your favorite food.

3. Did you listen to the selection on tape? If so, why do you think the author told about a celebration in America and one in Japan?

Can one phone call change everything?
Read how the Austin family copes with a crisis.

The Telephone Call

The Austins were a happy family with four children and two dogs. Late one night, the telephone rang. It was very bad news. Uncle Hal, a pilot, had died in a plane crash. His copilot had also died.

The next day Uncle Hal's wife and the copilot's daughter came to stay with the Austins. Vicky Austin had to give up her bed to Maggy, the copilot's daughter. Maggy was now an orphan and would stay with the Austins for a while.

Vicky wished she could tell Aunt Elena how sorry she was about Uncle Hal. When she looked at Aunt Elena, Vicky felt so sad she couldn't speak. On the other hand, her brother John was tactful and always seemed to know just what to say. Vicky tried to like Maggy. But the little girl was loud and ran around the house, knocking over chairs. Maggy told Vicky she wasn't as pretty as her sister and called her bossy.

That night Vicky, John, and their mother went outside to look at the sky. They talked about what had happened to Uncle Hal and Maggy's father. John asked why people have to die. He wished that things could always stay the same. Mother said that change is a part of life. Vicky prayed that her family could stay well. As they watched the night sky, she realized there were things she would never understand.

What Do You Think?

1. How would you feel if you were Vicky or John? Discuss your ideas with a friend.

2. Retell an important event in the story using the words below. Illustrate the last scene of the story.

   sky   die   understand

3. Did you listen to the story on tape? If so, how do you think Vicky will treat Maggy the next day? What makes you think this way?

Do you believe a pet crow could outwit a person?
Read to learn about these clever birds.

A Trouble-Making Crow

The George family had many wild animals as pets. Over the years these included a fox, a robin, three skunks, and four crows. One of the crows was named New York. Crows remember people who hurt them. A little girl had hurt New York, so he tried to hurt her. Mrs. George had to take New York to a park and set him free.

The family's next crow was named Crowbar. He tapped on the window to wake the children in the morning. He walked with them to the bus stop. When the bus took the children to school, Crowbar flew back to the kitchen window. The George family taught Crowbar to talk. Some people were scared when they heard him talk.

One time, Crowbar wanted to play with the George children. They were sliding down a slide in the yard. Crows can't slide because their feet have pads that hold them on perches. Crowbar watched the children for a while. He flew to the slide and tried to slide down, but his feet stuck to the board. Then he picked up a can lid from the sandbox and carried it to the top of the slide. Crowbar slid down on the lid!

After two years, many crows came into the yard. They called to Crowbar. They came for five days in a row. On the last day, Crowbar flew away with them. The George family was sorry to see him go.

What Do You Think?

1. Some people say wild animals are not good pets. What would the George family say to those people?

2. Find the word that means "to get the better of by being more intelligent." Have you ever been able to do this to someone? Explain. Make an illustration that shows what happened.

3. Did you listen to the selection on tape? If so, what facts can you add about what crows can do?

Could a hatchet save your life?
Read to find out how a boy survives in the wilderness.

From a Spark

Brian was flying to northern Canada to visit his father. The pilot of the small plane he was riding in had a heart attack and died. Brian had to land the plane. Then he was alone in the wilderness. His only tool was a hatchet.

Brian picked wild berries to eat. He found a cave to sleep in. But the cave was dark and cold. He needed to build a fire but had no matches. When an animal came into the cave, Brian threw the hatchet. It missed the animal, but hit a rock. Brian saw sparks. He realized he could use the hatchet to make a fire.

It took a long time to make the fire. Brian tried many times. He first tried tapping sparks onto dried grass. The sparks died out quickly. He tried twigs, and then grass and twigs together. The sparks sputtered and died. He then pulled strips of bark from trees for the fire. Brian used the hatchet to cut the bark into thin slivers. He tore up a twenty-dollar bill that was in his pocket and threw the pieces on the pile of bark. Again he hit the hatchet on the rock to make sparks. The sparks landed on the pile of bark, but the fire ignited and burned out quickly. He realized that he had to blow on the fire to keep it going.

Finally Brian made a fire that kept burning. The fire would help scare away animals. It would give light and keep him warm. He knew the fire was his friend.

What Do You Think?

1. Think about what might happen next in the story. What do you think Brian will do the next day?

2. Retell the most important scene in the story using the words below. Make an illustration to show what happened.

spark   **hatchet**   **ignite**

3. Did you listen to the story on tape? If so, what else did you learn about how to build a fire?

© Scott Foresman 6

Could a dust storm blow a special person into your life?
Read about a storm that did just that.

Storm-a-Dust

It had not rained for a long time. Lindy's father feared the crops would die. Suddenly a big flock of birds flew by, and then there was an eerie silence. Lindy saw a dark cloud coming their way. It was a dust storm. Lindy and her parents ran into the house.

From inside the house they saw a boy. He looked like a stick figure against the wall of dust. He was running in front of the dust storm. They let him in the house just as the storm came. Dust filled the house. It was hard to breathe. They held wet rags to their mouths to keep the dust out.

After the storm passed, they gave the boy some water and helped him sit up. He said his name was Drylongso. He had been working in the fields when the storm came. Everyone started to run and he had gotten lost.

Drylongso said he got his name because he was born during a drought, or a time without rain. His mother said wherever he went, life would grow better. Drylongso knew a lot about dust storms and what causes them. He said people should plant sunflowers to hold down the soil. He told some jokes about dust storms. "A pilot's plane got stuck in a black blizzard-a-dust, thousands of feet up. He bailed out. Had to shovel his way clear to the ground. When he got down, he carved a car for himself, blizzard black of dust, and drove away." Everyone laughed and began to feel a little bit better.

The next day Lindy, her parents, and Drylongso went outside. It was even hotter and drier than before. The corn was dying in the field. The tomato plants were covered with dust. Lindy and her mother started to sweep the dust out of the house.

What Do You Think?

1. Think about where the story takes place. How would this story be different if it took place in a big city?

2. Find the word that means "strange and scary." Has anything ever felt this way to you? Explain.

3. Did you listen to the story on tape? If so, do you feel a person like Drylongso could really exist? Explain why you feel as you do.

© Scott Foresman 6

Laura Perryman saves a giant sea turtle! How does she do it?
Read to find out.

The Day of the Turtle

Laura Perryman was fourteen years old in 1907. She lived on an island off the coast of England. In her diary she wrote about a special time when she found a giant sea turtle stuck in the sand on his back. The turtle was as big as her bed. He was too heavy to push or carry to the sea. He would die soon. Laura wanted to save the turtle. She knew people in her village would eat the turtle if they found him.

Laura saw specks of blood where the turtle had been pecked by seagulls. Laura threw pebbles at the gulls to make them go away. Laura found a broken *spar,* or mast from a ship, that had washed up on the beach. She used the spar as a lever to turn the turtle over. She covered the turtle with seaweed and driftwood to keep the birds away.

The next day Laura dug a path from the turtle to the sea. The path filled with water. When the tide came in, the turtle was only five yards from the sea. He tried to move but was too weak.

Laura realized the turtle was hungry. Her grandmother came to help. They tried feeding the turtle shrimp and seaweed. He refused to eat. Finally they gave the turtle some jellyfish. He ate them and seemed to feel stronger. He began to move slowly. Little by little he made his way down the path to the sea. When he reached the water, he swam away. Laura was both happy and sad. She missed the turtle. But she and Granny May now shared a secret. They had saved the turtle's life.

What Do You Think?

1. Describe the steps Laura takes to save the turtle.

2. Retell the story using the words below. Make an illustration of Laura and her grandmother helping the turtle.

   turtle   spar   jellyfish

3. Did you listen to the story on tape? If so, what details can you add about the setting of this story?

*Prince William Sound was full of plants and animals.
An oil spill changed all of that. What can be done?*

Saving the Sound

Prince William Sound was a beautiful body of water in Alaska. The Sound is 15,000 square miles—about twice the size of the state of New Jersey. Many plants and animals lived there. In 1989 an oil tanker, the *Exxon Valdez,* hit a reef in the Sound. About 11 million gallons of oil spilled into the water. This was the worst oil spill in the history of the United States.

No one was prepared for such a large oil spill. There are few roads in the area. Most places can be reached only by boat or plane. Ten hours passed before help came. By then the oil had spread out for miles like a thick, black, deadly wave. Fishermen tried to scoop up the oil in buckets. By the third day, the oil covered 100 square miles. The coastline was coated in thick, gooey slime.

The oil killed birds, otters, and other animals. Within a week after the spill, thousands of dead birds littered the beaches. Many had drowned because the heavy oil coated their feathers. Rescue workers tried to clean off the oil from animals that survived the spill. All fishing had to stop in contaminated areas. Many people in the area catch fish to earn a living. The oil spill changed their lives as well.

Since the accident, scientists have studied what happened. They learned what oil can do to the environment. They hope to learn how to clean up oil spills quickly. With time, Prince William Sound may return to what it once was.

What Do You Think?

1. What were the effects of the oil spill on living things? Share some facts you learned with your friends or family.

2. Find the word that means "made impure" or "polluted." What does something polluted look like? Make an illustration that shows something before the spill and the same thing after the spill.

3. Did you listen to the selection on tape? If so, would you be interested in helping clean up an oil spill? How would you help?

© Scott Foresman 6

Who was the first woman doctor in the United States?
Find out about a woman who wouldn't take no for an answer.

Elizabeth Blackwell: Medical Pioneer

"Elizabeth Blackwell: Medical Pioneer" is a play about a brave woman who stood up to social rules to become the first female doctor in the United States. In 1847 Elizabeth Blackwell was 25 years old. At this time most women got married, stayed home, and raised a family. But Elizabeth wanted to be a surgeon. People told her that women could be only nurses.

Elizabeth studied with Dr. Barnes for three years. She asked for his help in going to medical school. But even with his help, she was turned down by 25 schools. No one thought a woman was qualified to be a doctor. Finally she was admitted to Geneva Medical College in New York. Elizabeth graduated with honors and moved to Paris. But, even though she had a medical degree, no hospital would hire her as a doctor. She had to work as a nurse after all.

Elizabeth worked at a maternity hospital in Paris. One night she was called to help a sick baby. The baby had an infection in its eyes. Elizabeth caught the infection herself, which left her blind in one eye. She had to give up her dream of becoming a surgeon.

Elizabeth returned to America. Still no hospital would hire her as a doctor. She opened a clinic in a poor part of New York City. Her medical ideas shocked some people. She said fresh air, exercise, and a balanced diet would help keep people well. She worked around the clock seeing patients. Elizabeth Blackwell continued her fight to open people's minds to change.

What Do You Think?

1. Think about how Elizabeth Blackwell acted when things didn't go her way. What words would you use to describe her character?

2. Retell the selection using the words below. Make an illustration of an important event in Elizabeth Blackwell's life.

   surgeon   **qualified**   **infection**

3. Did you listen to the play on tape? If so, what else did you learn about Elizabeth Blackwell's fight to become a doctor?

Read about two cousins who are partners.
Which one will grow up to be the better person?

Born Worker

José's father worked for the telephone company, climbing poles and fixing wires. His mother worked at a sewing machine all day. José knew he would be a laborer too.

José's cousin Arnie did not like hard work. His parents had good jobs in offices. They gave Arnie everything he wanted. When the boys were in junior high, Arnie had an idea to make money. Arnie's plan was that he would find jobs, and José would do the work.

Arnie did find jobs, and José worked hard. One day a man named Mr. Clemens hired them to clean his swimming pool. It was very dirty. José scrubbed and scrubbed. Arnie sat on the side of the pool and watched. Later Mr. Clemens came out to see how the work was going. Suddenly he fell into the empty pool and hit his head. José rushed over to help the man. He told Arnie to call 911. Instead, Arnie left.

José called 911. He put ice on Mr. Clemens's head. A fire truck came to help Mr. Clemens. Just then Arnie reappeared and said he had been the one scrubbing the pool when the man fell. José just walked away. He knew he and Arnie were different kinds of people. José was more than just a good worker. He was a good person.

What Do You Think?

1. Think about what kind of people José and Arnie are. Do you think they will continue to be partners?

2. Find the word that means "a person who does work requiring much physical labor." What kind of job would you rather do? Explain. Make an illustration that shows you doing the job.

3. Did you listen to the story on tape? If so, what can you add about the differences between José and Arnie?

© Scott Foresman 6

Could a child with polio grow up to compete in the Olympics?
Read about Wilma who never stopped believing in herself.

Wilma Unlimited

Wilma Rudolph was born in 1940 in Clarksville, Tennessee. She was a small baby and was often sick. Her mother cared for her at home. Her family could not afford constant doctor care, and only one doctor in Clarksville would treat black people.

Before she turned five, Wilma got polio. In those days, many children with polio died. Those who survived usually walked with crutches for the rest of their lives. Wilma's left leg twisted inward, and she had to wear a brace on it. Twice a week she and her mother rode the bus to the nearest hospital that would treat black patients, 50 miles away in Nashville.

At school Wilma had to watch the other children play from the sidelines. She did exercises to make her leg stronger. One day at church, Wilma took off her brace and was able to walk a little. By the time she was 12, she no longer needed the brace.

After years of sitting on the sidelines, Wilma couldn't wait to play basketball. She was still skinny, but no longer tiny. She was the star of her team in high school, and she won an athletic scholarship to college. There she began running races. In 1960, Wilma went to Rome for the Olympics. She won three gold medals. Wilma Rudolph had once been told she would never walk again. Now she was the fastest woman in the world!

What Do You Think?

1. Think about the title of this selection. What limits were placed on Wilma Rudolph from an early age?

2. Retell the story using the words below. Make an illustration of an important event in Wilma Rudolph's life.

   unlimited   **athletic**   **polio**

3. Did you listen to the selection on tape? If so, what else did you learn about how Wilma Rudolph overcame her problems?

© Scott Foresman 6

The Mudville baseball team seems sure to lose the game.
Will their best hitter save the day?

Casey at the Bat

"Casey at the Bat" is a famous poem about a baseball game. Mudville team was losing. The score was four to two with one inning left to play. The first two Mudville batters were thrown out at first base. Then Flynn hit a single. Blake followed him and hit a double. With two runners on base, it was Casey's turn at bat. Now everything depended on Casey.

The fans yelled loudly as Casey came up to bat. He looked proud, and he was smiling. He took his time. First he lifted his hat to the crowd. They clapped when he rubbed dirt on his hands and then wiped them on his shirt. As Casey held up his bat, he looked defiant and a sneer curled his lip.

The pitcher threw the first pitch. Casey let the ball go by. "Strike one," said the umpire. The fans yelled, "Kill the umpire!" Casey raised his hand to quiet the crowd. He smiled and signaled the pitcher to throw again. Another pitch went by and again Casey did not swing. The umpire called, "Strike two!"

Casey's face grew stern and cold. The crowd knew Casey would not let the next pitch go by. But when Casey swung at the ball, he missed. The Mudville fans had to go home in despair. Mighty Casey had struck out.

What Do You Think?

1. Were you surprised by the ending? Why or why not?

2. Find the word in the summary that means "hopeless feeling." Have you ever felt hopeless? Explain.

3. Did you listen to the poem on tape? If so, what words can you add to describe the Mudville team and fans?

Harriet has a crush on Mars.
But why is her model of the solar system falling apart?

The Night of the Pomegranate

Each member of Harriet's class had to make a model of the solar system. Harriet's model was a mess. The sun and the nine planets were made out of rolled-up balls of newspaper. They were mounted on a piece of green cardboard. The tape kept coming loose. When she ran out of glue, Harriet used chewing gum.

Yet Harriet was interested in the solar system. She loved Mars! Her brother even said she had a crush on Mars. This month Mars was close to Earth in its orbit. Harriet and her friend Mrs. Pond had watched Mars every night. That's why she hadn't spent enough time on her model.

Harriet's classmates had models that looked good. Some of the kids had models purchased from the hobby store. The planets were all the right sizes and nicely painted. Wires held the sun and planets in place.

The students showed their models to the class. When it was Harriet's turn, she knew her model looked bad. She could tell that her teacher thought it was unsatisfactory. But as Harriet began to talk about Mars, her teacher realized Harriet knew a lot about the solar system. Harriet compared the size of Mars to a pomegranate seed. She told the class about watching Mars with Mrs. Pond. She had learned more by looking at Mars than by making a model.

What Do You Think?

1. Have you ever learned more by doing something than by reading about it? Tell a friend about your experience.

2. Retell the story using the words below. Make an illustration of your favorite scene.

   learned   **model**   **Mars**

3. Did you listen to the story on tape? If so, what can you add about Harriet's friendship with Mrs. Pond?

If you saw someone wearing face paint, what would you think? Read about this Native American tradition.

Spring Paint

Part of Joseph Bruchac's heritage is Native American tales. One tells about the seasons. In the tale, Old Man Winter is visited by a young man. The young man's face is painted with red lines and circles that look like the sun. Everything begins to melt. The young man sends Old Man Winter away so spring can begin.

Another part of Joseph Bruchac's heritage is what his grandfather taught him about nature. When Bruchac was a boy, his grandfather taught him about plants, animals, and rocks. Grandpa said the woods was a place where Joseph could be safe, as long as he understood what was around him.

Joseph's favorite plant was the bloodroot. His grandfather said when the bloodroot plant blossomed in the woods, spring would soon come. Each April they would look for the plant together. Grandpa would take the stem and make red lines and circles on Joseph's face. He called it "spring paint," and said it would keep bugs away.

The bloodroot plant was used in this way by the Native American people of the area many years ago. It was also used as a dye for clothing and baskets. Some of these people were Joseph Bruchac's ancestors. His grandfather was keeping a tradition alive.

What Do You Think?

1. Joseph Bruchac's grandfather taught him about spring paint. How can Bruchac pass along this tradition?

2. Find the word that means "persons from whom you are descended, such as grandparents and great-grandparents." What do you know about your grandparents? Did they share any traditions with you? Explain.

3. Did you listen to the selection on tape? If so, do you think the things Joseph Bruchac learned from his grandfather are important? Explain why you feel as you do.

© Scott Foresman 6

Suppose you made a promise to someone who later died.
Would you keep that promise?

A Brother's Promise

In the 1880s France was planning to give a gift to the United States. The gift was the Statue of Liberty. The hand and torch were already in New York City. But a pedestal was needed for the statue to stand on. No money had been raised for the pedestal, so the rest of the statue stayed in France.

Annie and her older brother, Geoffrey, went to see the hand and torch. They climbed up in the torch and looked through Geoffrey's spyglass. They made a promise that they would return to the torch when the statue was put together. Annie had an awful feeling that something terrible was going to happen. Soon afterward, Geoffrey went back to art school in Paris.

A year later Geoffrey was killed in a car accident. His friend sent Annie the spyglass. Annie sold the spyglass and sent the money to the pedestal fund. In her letter she said the money was sent in her brother's memory. Her letter was published in the newspaper. As a result, many other people decided to give money in memory of relatives. Finally there was enough money to build the pedestal.

When the statue arrived, there was a big celebration. The newspaper publisher called Annie to the front of the crowd. He gave her back Geoffrey's spyglass and thanked her for her help. Then Annie climbed up in the torch. She looked through the spyglass and remembered the promise she and Geoffrey had made.

What Do You Think?

1. Why is it important for Annie to keep the promise?

2. Retell the story using the words below. Make an illustration to show an important event in the story.

   spyglass   **pedestal**   **fund**   **promise**

3. Did you listen to the story on tape? If so, what else did you learn about the Statue of Liberty?

Do you know what your life's work will be? Read about a boy who "caught blacksmith fever" and made his dream come true.

from Catching the Fire

The great-grandson of slaves, Philip Simmons grew up in Charleston, South Carolina. He began working as a blacksmith when he was 13 years old.

A blacksmith uses fire to soften iron so it can be hammered and shaped into forms, such as ornamental gates, fences, and railings. This craft is over 5,000 years old. It started in ancient Africa. Philip had to learn to operate the bellows, which is a leather lung that forces air into the forge to keep the fire hot. He started out by repairing tools and making horseshoes. When he was older, he began making gates out of wrought iron. He used traditional patterns as well as new patterns he designed. He was the first African American blacksmith to forge animal figures.

In 1972, a young man named John Michael Vlach came into Philip Simmons's workshop. He asked about the history of blacksmithing. They took a tour of Charleston, and Simmons showed Vlach some of the gates he had made. John Vlach realized that Philip Simmons was not just a blacksmith. He was an artist.

Four years later, Vlach invited Simmons to show his work at the Festival of American Folklife in Washington, D.C. Many people came to see Simmons as he worked. He created a beautiful gate with stars, a moon, and a fish. That gate is now part of the Smithsonian Institution.

Today Philip Simmons is an honored artist, teacher, and businessman. His gates, fences, and railings can be seen all over Charleston. Several of his works are in museums.

What Do You Think?

1. What words would you use to describe Philip Simmons, based on the events in his life?

2. Retell the selection using the words below. Make an illustration of an important event in Philip Simmons's life.

   blacksmith　　　　**workshop**　　　　**artist**

3. Did you listen to the selection on tape? If so, what did you learn about the history of blacksmithing?

What are the Seven Wonders of the Ancient World?
Read to find out about these incredible structures.

The Seven Wonders of the Ancient World

Over 2,000 years ago, people wrote about seven amazing buildings and structures they had heard of or seen. All were found in a small area around the Mediterranean Sea. These became known as the Seven Wonders of the Ancient World.

Who built these Wonders and why were they created? The Great Pyramid at Giza is the oldest of the Seven Wonders. It is also the only one still standing today. It was built as a tomb for a pharaoh, or king, of ancient Egypt.

What we know of the other six Wonders is based mainly on writings and drawings. As archaeologists excavate buried cities, they learn more about these structures.

King Nebuchadnezzar II had the Hanging Gardens of Babylon built to remind his wife of her homeland. The Temple of Artemis at Ephesus was built to honor the goddess of the moon. The Statue of Zeus at Olympia stood 43 feet high. The Mausoleum at Halicarnassus was a huge tomb built for a ruler named Mausolus. The Colossus of Rhodes was a giant statue made of bronze. The Pharos of Alexandria was the world's first lighthouse. It took 20 years to build.

What Do You Think?

1. We know six of the Seven Wonders existed only because people wrote about them. What modern Wonder, such as the Eiffel Tower, could you write about?

2. Find the word that means "scientists who study the people, customs, and life of ancient times." What do you think scientists in the future will think about our customs?

3. Did you listen to the selection on tape? If so, how were the Seven Wonders alike?

What is more valuable than gold?
Read about a thief who discovers true riches.

The Gold Coin

Juan was a thief. He stole things at night and hid during the day. One night he saw an old woman through the window of her hut. She held a gold coin in her hand. He heard her say to herself that she must be the richest person in the world. Juan hid in the bushes. When the old woman left, he searched her hut for the gold, but he couldn't find it.

He followed the path the old woman had taken and came to a farm. When he arrived, she had just left. He found out her name was Doña Josefa, and she helped sick people. Then she offered them a gold coin. The farmers told Juan they would help him find Doña Josefa if he would help them finish their work. Then they led him to another farm where she had been. She had just left, and again Juan was asked to work in exchange for help in finding her. In this way, Juan followed the old woman from farm to farm, always just missing her.

After many days and much hard work, Juan found Doña Josefa. She still had the gold coin. None of the sick people she had offered it to would take it. They always said someone else would need it more. She offered Juan the coin. He was stunned. When a girl came to ask Doña Josefa for help with a newborn baby, Juan gave back the coin. He said the baby would need it more than he did. He offered to fix Doña Josefa's roof. He had learned that helping others was more valuable than gold.

What Do You Think?

1. What message do you think the author is trying to give? Share ideas with a friend.

2. Find the word that means "shocked or dazed." Why do you think Juan felt this way when Doña Josefa gave him the coin?

3. Did you listen to the story on tape? If so, what can you add about how Juan changed from the beginning of the story to the end?

© Scott Foresman 6

Would you like to travel by dogsled to the North Pole? Read about some explorers who made the trip.

To the Pole!

In 1994, six people headed for the North Pole. They traveled from Russia by dogsled, crossing frozen snow and floating ice. They camped at the Pole. Then they started south by canoe, heading for Canada. During the trip they communicated by computer with students around the world. The purpose of their trip was to help people learn about pollution in the Arctic. *To the Pole!* is a journal of the explorers' strenuous but educational trip.

The leader of the expedition was Will Steger. One of the biggest problems was getting across "leads," or rivers of water that appeared when the ice broke apart. Leads could be as wide as a football field. The explorers would have to put their dogsleds on rafts of ice and pull them across by ropes.

There were 22 dogs divided into three teams. One time a sled fell through the ice. The explorers had to break up the ice while the dogs worked to pull the sled out of the water.

The group gathered snow samples for scientists to study. They found that pollution from cities travels through ocean currents to the Arctic. Fish become contaminated. The fish are eaten by seals, and the seals are then eaten by polar bears. Even humans have been affected by this pollution, which comes from thousands of miles away.

What Do You Think?

1. If you went on a trip like the one described, what would you find most difficult? Explain.

2. Retell something important about what you read using the words below. Make an illustration that shows one of the challenges the explorers faced.

   Arctic   expedition   pollution

3. Did you listen to the selection on tape? If so, how did the team live during the trip?

What if your family had to leave immediately for a faraway place? Find out how one family survived a difficult journey.

from El Güero: A True Adventure Story

In 1876, a boy called El Güero and his family had to leave their home in Mexico City. A new president had seized control of Mexico. El Güero's father, a judge, was exiled by the new president. He was being sent to faraway Baja California. The wealthy family had to leave in a hurry and could take only a few things. El Güero and his little sister, Maruca, had to say good-by to their beloved pets.

The family consisted of El Güero, his parents, Maruca, and his aunt, Tía Vicky. They traveled by horses and mules to Acapulco. They ate around a campfire and slept outdoors or in huts. After three days they were stopped by bandits. One of the bandits knew the judge. The bandits offered to protect the family as they traveled.

It was cold as they traveled through the mountains. Then they came to the hot plains. Maruca became ill with a fever.

When they finally reached Acapulco, they got medicine for Maruca and stayed until she was well. Then the family got on a ship headed for San Diego. After many days on board, the captain said the family must get off the ship. The sailors took the family in rowboats to the shore of Cabo San Lucas. The family lived on the beach for about a month until another ship came. The captain of this ship promised to take them to San Diego. El Güero's family was relieved to be rescued at last!

What Do You Think?

1. Think about the long journey El Güero's family made. What do you think were the most difficult parts of the trip?

2. Find the word that means "forced to leave one's country or home." What do you think it would be like to be forced to leave your home or country?

3. Did you listen to the selection on tape? If so, how did El Güero's family members change during the trip?

Fasten your seat belt—you are headed for Mars!
Read to find out what the trip will be like.

Destination: Mars

What would it be like to be on a spaceship that is heading for Mars? Imagine that you are among the first humans to visit another planet. Your mission is to look for signs of life on Mars.

The trip will take six months. Then you will have to wait eighteen months before it is safe to come home. The return trip will take another six months. You will not see your family again for almost three years.

There is no air on Mars, and no water. The gravity is one third the gravity on Earth. If you weighed 80 pounds on Earth, you would weigh 30 pounds on Mars. This difference in gravity can make your body weak.

When you land, you and the other crew members will look for signs of life in the form of fossils. You will have a rover to drive. You must explore the dry rivers and lake beds. Fossils on Earth are hard to detect, and it will be even harder on Mars. It's possible that there has never been life on Mars.

But you and your group will be proof that life can exist on Mars. You will set up greenhouses to see what plants can be grown without soil. You will study Martian weather and geology. You will begin preparing Mars for the next group who comes. One day, perhaps people will form a permanent colony on Mars.

What Do You Think?

1. What is the purpose of the trip to Mars? Do you think the mission will be successful?

2. Find the word that means "find or discover evidence of something." Have you ever found a fossil or seen a picture of one? Make an illustration of a fossil that might be found on Mars and what you think the creature that left it looked like.

3. Did you listen to the selection on tape? If so, what is life like on the spaceship?

Milo was always bored. Find out how a ticking watchdog named Tock rescued him from the Doldrums.

The Land of Expectations

Milo was bored. He sat in his room and looked at all of his toys and books and tools. Suddenly he saw a giant package, addressed to him. Inside was a tollbooth kit, which included coins for paying tolls, a book of rules, and a map. Milo put the tollbooth together. He looked at the map and chose the town of Dictionopolis as his destination. He got into his toy electric car and rode up to the tollbooth. He put in a coin and found himself on a highway. What had started as make-believe was now real.

A sign said that Milo was in the land of Expectations. As Milo headed toward the town of Dictionopolis, he began daydreaming. Not paying attention, he took a wrong turn. He drove mile after mile. The countryside lost all its color. He was in the Doldrums, a place where nothing ever happens and nothing ever changes. The people there were called the Lethargarians. They did nothing all day. Milo's car came to a stop and would not go on.

Milo met a watchdog named Tock. Tock had a large alarm clock for a body. Milo and the dog got into the car. Tock told Milo he must start thinking to make the car run again. Milo thought hard, and the car began to move. As they drove along, they began to see colors again. Together they drove toward the town of Dictionopolis.

What Do You Think?

1. Milo goes to places with interesting names. Make up a name for a place Milo might visit. Describe what that place would be like.

2. Retell the story using the words below. Make an illustration to show an important event in the story.

   expectations   **tollbooth**   **destination**

3. Did you listen to the story on tape? If so, what do you know about Tock the watchdog?

What would it be like to join a cattle drive?
Read about how an escaped slave learns to be a cowboy.

The Trail Drive

In 1863, Midnight was thirteen years old. His parents helped him escape from slavery. He rode on his horse to Mexico, where he met an African American cowboy named Mississippi Slim. Slim helped him get a job on a cattle drive.

Midnight's job was to take care of the *remuda,* or the spare horses. He had to lead and care for the six horses the other cowboys weren't riding. The days were long and hot. Midnight and the other cowboys rode for hours and hours. Each day was like another. When they stopped to eat and sleep, Midnight tied the horses to a picket line.

One day they came to the Red River. The water was deep, and Midnight had to make sure the horses didn't take a bad step and break a leg. Midnight led the horses splashing into the river. The water rushed all around them, but Midnight brought the horses across safely. The other cowboys followed, leading the cattle through the water.

That night Midnight was very tired. A noise that sounded like screaming woke him from a dream. There was a cougar stalking the campsite. The cougar came back every night for a week. Midnight realized the cougar was after the horses. Midnight threw a rock at the cougar, and the big cat pounced on him. He wrestled with the animal and got badly clawed. But he scared the cougar off and saved the horses.

What Do You Think?

1. What words would you use to describe Midnight's character based on the way he does his job? Share your ideas with a friend.

2. Find the word that means "moving cattle across land." What do you think it would be like to do this? Explain. Make an illustration that shows what your job would be.

3. Did you listen to the story on tape? If so, what else did you learn about Midnight's job?

Boy saves wedding from disaster! Read how Noah turned a visit to his grandparents into a great vacation.

Noah Writes a B & B Letter

When Noah's parents went on a cruise, Noah stayed with his grandparents in Florida. They lived in a place called Century Village. Century Village was not like any place Noah had been. Almost everyone who lived there was retired.

Two of the people who lived in Century Village were getting married. The people of Century Village called a meeting in the clubhouse to organize the wedding. Everyone on the wedding committee offered to help in some way. Noah learned calligraphy, the art of beautiful handwriting, and helped address the wedding invitations.

Noah also helped make a grocery list for the wedding. On the day of the wedding, Noah carried plants and food to the clubhouse. He delivered flowers to the bride and groom. But when he tried to move the wedding cake in the wagon, there was an accident. The best man tripped over the wagon handle and broke his ankle. Noah offered to be best man instead. He wore a T-shirt painted to look like a tuxedo.

When Noah returned home, his mother told him to write a B & B letter to his grandparents. B & B stands for "bread and butter." It is a letter written to thank people for having you as their houseguest. But Noah felt his grandparents should thank him. After all, he had saved the day! But Noah also remembered his new friends, his calligraphy lessons, and the gifts he received. He realized he really was thankful for the experiences he had.

What Do You Think?

1. How do you think Noah should begin his thank-you letter to his grandparents? Write the first three sentences.

2. Find the word that means "group of people appointed to do a special thing." How could you have helped the people who were planning the wedding?

3. Did you listen to the story on tape? If so, what gifts did Noah give?

© Scott Foresman 6

Can bad fortune lead to good things? Read how blindness led one boy to make the world a better place.

Louis Braille

Louis Braille was born in 1809 in France. An accident in his father's workshop left Louis blind at age five. A priest offered to teach Louis, who was a quick learner. Louis learned to find his way around his village using a cane. He was later able to attend school with the other children in his village. That was unheard of in those days. Louis had a good memory and was usually at the top of his class.

In the 1800s there were few schools for the blind. There was no way to teach them to read or write. Blind people were often thought of as stupid. When Louis was ten, he left for the National Institute for Blind Youth in Paris. It was the only school for the blind in France.

The few books at the school were written with large letters that students felt with their fingers. It took a long time to read just one sentence. In 1819, Charles Barbier had invented a system of dots and dashes punched into paper to help soldiers communicate at night. Louis heard Barbier give a talk about his system. He thought the Barbier system was too complicated. Louis invented his own system using only six dots. The dots were raised rather than punched into the paper. The system was easy to learn and enabled blind people to write as well as read.

Louis became a teacher at the Institute. He learned to play the piano and organ. The Braille system is used throughout the world today.

What Do You Think?

1. Do you think Louis Braille was a hero? Why or why not?

2. Retell the selection using the words below. Use the Braille alphabet above to write your name.

   invented   **communicate**   **complicated**

3. Did you listen to the selection on tape? If so, why was the Braille system ignored for many years?

© Scott Foresman 6

How would you estimate the distance around the Earth? Find out who made the first accurate map of the world.

The Librarian Who Measured the Earth

Eratosthenes was born more than two thousand years ago. He lived in a Greek city on the northern coast of Africa. Even as a baby, he was curious and full of wonder. He loved school because he could ask questions there. He was very good at math, but his favorite subject was geography.

When he was older, Eratosthenes went to Athens to learn more. He began making lists and writing books. When Eratosthenes was thirty years old, the king of Egypt hired him as his son's tutor. Eratosthenes moved to the city of Alexandria, which was the center of all learning at that time. He enjoyed going to the Alexandria museum and library. When the head librarian died, Eratosthenes was asked to take his place.

By this time people knew the Earth was round. Eratosthenes wanted to know how big the Earth was. How could such a large object be measured? He figured out a way to use geometry to measure the circumference, or distance around the middle of the Earth. He took the distance between the cities of Alexandria and Syene and multiplied by 50 to estimate the distance around the Earth. He calculated the circumference of the Earth to be 24,662 miles. This is only about 200 miles different from the number we use today. His measurements provided the first accurate map of the world. Eratosthenes' first geography book of the world was now complete.

What Do You Think?

1. Eratosthenes was always very curious. How do you think this trait shaped his life and work?

2. Find the word that means "make a careful guess about amount, size, or value." How would you guess a friend's height? Explain. Make an illustration to show your method.

3. Did you listen to the selection on tape? If so, why was Alexandria known as a center for learning?

Can an eight-legged alien teach a human to play the flute?
Read how two very different musicians find common ground.

Tyree's Song

Most Earth colonists on the planet Harmony left the city of Old Sion when it flooded. Those who remained were known as Silkies. A young man named Tyree learned to play music from his friend Jubal. Tyree's father was the leader of the Silkies. He thought it was undignified for his son to be a musician. He ordered Tyree to stop making music.

Tyree was determined to continue making music on his homemade flute. He rowed a boat to one of the abandoned mansions in Sheol. Sheol was home to the Argans, who lived on Harmony before the Earth colonists came. No Silkie would hear his music there because no Silkie would go there.

Tyree began to play his flute. Then he heard strange and lovely music. The musician was Amadeus, an old Argan songsmith with eight arm-legs.

Amadeus agreed to teach Tyree to play Argan music. Tyree secretly visited Sheol three times a week for his music lessons. Little by little he learned more about Argan music. One night Amadeus arranged for Tyree to play his flute for a group of Argans. The Argans made fun of Tyree at first. To calm his anxiety, he played a human song in the Argan style. The Argans were stunned. Then Tyree and Amadeus played an Argan song together. Their song echoed through the abandoned streets of Old Sion.

What Do You Think?

1. What do you think Tyree will do next? Discuss your ideas with a friend.

2. Retell the story using the words below. Make an illustration of a key event.

   colonists　　　**music**　　　**anxiety**

3. Did you listen to the story on tape? If so, what interesting facts about Argan music did you learn?

Cutters, Carvers, and the Cathedral

The Cathedral of Saint John the Divine is in New York City. Work on the cathedral started in 1892. It took fifty years to finish the main body of the church. Then World War II began, and no work was done for thirty years. At that time, master stone carvers were invited from Europe to train young people from the neighborhood to become masons and carvers.

It took many people to build the cathedral: architects, engineers, carpenters, glass makers, electricians, masons, and rock cutters. Most of the limestone for the cathedral came from Indiana. There the quarry workers cut giant blocks of limestone from the earth. The blocks were transported to New York on flatbed trucks.

Masons used patterns to shape each block of stone. Carvers cut intricate decorations that would be part of the finished cathedral. The men and women who worked on the cathedral came from the neighborhood and from other countries as well. They formed a community of workers.

Simon Verity was the master carver. He used a hammer and chisel to create beautiful designs and figures for the cathedral. He said that his work was less important than that of the masons, who shaped the blocks that hold the cathedral together.

Work on the cathedral has stopped for lack of money. Yet services, concerts, and festivals still take place.

What Do You Think?

1. Do you agree with Simon Verity's statement that the work of the masons is more important than the work of the master carver? Share what you learned with your friends or family.

2. Retell the selection using the words below. Make an illustration of something you would like to build out of stone.

   cathedral   **masons**   **carvers**

3. Did you listen to the selection on tape? If so, what kind of people chose to work on the cathedral?

© Scott Foresman 6

Selection Summary Answer Key

Tony and the Snark   p. 40

1. Possible answers: Tony thought he would buy a motorbike, but he bought a sailboat instead. Tony was surprised that his sailing teacher was a teenage girl. Tony thought he wouldn't enjoy his summer, but he did.

2. submerged; answers may vary

3. Possible answers: The town is on a peninsula. There is a statue of the town's founder, Captain Ezra Littlejohn. The town was founded in 1731. There is a legend of a lost treasure.

Teammates   p. 41

1. The author seems to admire Jackie Robinson's talents and courage. The author writes positive things about Robinson, such as how he controlled his anger and never gave up.

2. Answers will vary.

3. Robinson and Reese both played shortstop. Reese refused to sign a petition against Robinson. He was a good friend to Robinson.

April's Mud   p. 42

1. Her classmates liked her father and were interested in the adobe house.

2. Answers will vary.

3. Possible answers: April thought her mother was beautiful. She was embarrassed about living in a school bus. She was angry with her father for not telling her he would be coming to school.

Hot Dogs and Bamboo Shoots   p. 43

1. Yoshiko learned she was a mixture of two cultures because she went to Japan and saw how she was similar to and different from Japanese people.

2. traditional; answers will vary

3. The author wanted to show how celebrations in America and Japan are alike and different.

The Telephone Call   p. 44

1. Answers will vary. Students may say they would not like to give up their bedroom. They wouldn't know what to say to Aunt Elena and Maggy. They may say they would feel sorry for Maggy and want to help her.

2. Answers will vary.

3. Vicky will probably try to be friendlier to Maggy the next day. While she and John watch the stars with their mother, she thinks about her own family and how hard it would be to lose one of them. She knows Maggy has lost both her parents and realizes the little girl needs to be treated with kindness.

Selection Summary Answer Key

A Trouble-Making Crow   **p. 45**

1. The George family would probably say that wild animals can be dangerous, as when New York hurt the little girl. They can also be fun, but you must let them keep their freedom—as when they let Crowbar fly away with the other crows.

2. outwit, answers will vary

3. Possible answers: Crows can count, sulk, taunt other animals, communicate with each other, and recognize that a gun means death.

From a Spark   **p. 46**

1. Possible answers: Brian will look for more fuel to keep the fire burning. He will hunt for food that he can cook over the fire. He will use the fire to signal for help.

2. Answers will vary.

3. Possible answers: Only striking the hatchet a certain way against the rock will make sparks. The kindling must be very fine, like hairs. A fire needs oxygen to burn.

Storm-a-Dust   **p. 47**

1. Possible answers: The family might live in a tall building. There would be no crops to be ruined. There would be more people living close by.

2. eerie; answers will vary.

3. Answers will vary.

The Day of the Turtle   **p. 48**

1. Laura tried to turn the turtle over. She covered him to keep birds away. She dug a path to the sea. She and Granny May fed the turtle.

2. Answers will vary.

3. Possible answers: There were many storms. The high waves washed things onto the beach. Often there was fog. Many people earned their living from the sea.

Saving the Sound   **p. 49**

1. Possible answers: Birds and other animals were killed. Dead birds covered the beaches. Living animals were coated with oil. All fishing had to stop.

2. contaminated; answers will vary.

3. Answers will vary.

Elizabeth Blackwell: Medical Pioneer   **p. 50**

1. Possible answers: independent, determined, strong-willed, brave.

2. Answers will vary.

3. Possible answers: She worked as a music teacher to earn money for her education. She refused to dress as a man to study in Paris. She was called a lunatic.

© Scott Foresman 6

Selection Summary Answer Key

Born Worker   p. 51

1. Possible answers: No, they will not be partners because Arnie is lazy. Yes, but José will insist that Arnie take part in the work.

2. laborer; answers will vary.

3. Possible answers: Arnie wore fancier shoes than José. Arnie's family had taken exotic vacations. Arnie was good with words while José was good with his hands. José disliked asking for work while Arnie didn't mind.

Wilma Unlimited   p. 52

1. Wilma was tiny and sickly. Her family was not wealthy. Only one doctor in town would treat black people. She developed polio. The nearest hospital was 50 miles away.

2. Answers will vary.

3. Possible answers: She never gave up. She got around by hopping on one foot. She worked hard at her exercises so she could go to school.

Casey at the Bat   p. 53

1. Answers will vary.

2. despair

3. Possible answers: hopeful, worried, grim, stricken, defiant, haughty, unhappy.

The Night of the Pomegranate   p. 54

1. Answers will vary.

2. Answers will vary.

3. Possible answers: Mrs. Pond gave Harriet her first pomegranate. They drank cocoa to keep warm. Mrs. Pond told Harriet about *The War of the Worlds*.

Spring Paint   p. 55

1. Possible answers: He can pass along the tradition to his own children and grandchildren by telling them the tale and what he was taught about spring paint. He can share the tradition with others by writing about it.

2. ancestors; answers will vary.

3. Answers will vary.

A Brother's Promise   p. 56

1. Answer: Annie wants to keep the promise to honor her brother's memory.

2 Answers will vary.

3. Possible answers: Some people thought the statue was a hoax. The statue stands in New York Harbor. The torch symbolizes the light of freedom. A tablet on the statue says "July 4, 1776."

Selection Summary Answer Key

from Catching the Fire   p. 57

1. Possible answers: determined, hardworking, artistic, good businessman.

2. Answers will vary.

3. Possible answers: The craft is over 5,000 years old. Enslaved West Africans brought their blacksmith traditions to the United States. The leather bellows was replaced by the electric forge blower.

The Seven Wonders of the Ancient World   p. 58

1. Answers will vary. Students might name the Sears Tower, Mount Rushmore, the Taj Mahal, Disney World.

2. archaeologists; answers will vary.

3. Possible answers: All are from ancient times. All are in the same general area. All are gigantic structures. All took many years to build.

The Gold Coin   p. 59

1. Possible answers: It is better to give than to receive. There is always someone more in need than you.

2. stunned; answers will vary.

3. Possible answers: He learned the pleasure of sharing with others. He enjoyed being in the sunlight. His bent back straightened. He began to smile.

To the Pole!   p. 60

1. Possible answers: crossing leads, sleds falling through the ice, cold weather, dogs getting tired.

2. Answers will vary.

3. Possible answers: They slept in tents. They had to eat well to keep up their energy. They had to melt ice for soups and drinks. They rarely bathed or changed clothes.

from El Güero: A True Adventure Story   p. 61

1. Possible answers: traveling by mule, bad weather, Maruca's illness, being put off the first ship, living on the beach.

2. exiled; answers will vary.

3. Possible answers: El Güero and his father became closer. Tía Vicky became less worried about her appearance. Maruca grew stronger. El Güero grew taller.

Selection Summary Answer Key

Destination: Mars   p. 62

1. The purpose of the trip to Mars is to look for signs of life. Answers will vary for the second part of the question.

2. detect; answers will vary.

3. Possible answers: The astronauts have books on computer, movies, and music. They each have a small private space. They must add water to meals in packets. They float as they sleep. The toilet has a seat belt.

The Land of Expectations   p. 63

1. Answers will vary.

2. Answers will vary.

3. Possible answers: He's always making sure no one wastes time. He makes the sound *tickticktick*. His brother's name is Tick and makes the sound *tocktocktock*.

The Trail Drive   p. 64

1. Possible answers: hardworking, responsible, caring, brave.

2. drive; answers will vary.

3. Possible answers: He drove pickets, or stakes, into the ground. He tied a rope to the pickets, and then tethered the horses to the picket line. He had to take turns guarding the horses. He rode his own horse, Dahomey.

Noah Writes a B & B Letter   p. 65

1. Possible answer: Thank you for letting me stay with you at Century Village. I enjoyed helping prepare for the wedding. I'm glad I was able to step in and be the best man.

2. committee; answers will vary.

3. Possible answer: Noah gave his pen and ink, his T-shirt, a package of Post-it notes, and his wagon.

Louis Braille   p. 66

1. Answers will vary.

2. Answers will vary.

3. Possible answers: The heads of the Institute weren't blind and didn't understand how simple the Braille system was. They knew older systems and didn't want to learn a new one. Some people thought a system invented by a student not an inventor couldn't be very good.

The Librarian Who Measured the Earth   p. 67

1. His curiosity led him to do well in school, make lists, and write books. His questioning nature led him to the museum and library in Alexandria. As a librarian, his curiosity helped him figure out how to measure the distance around the Earth.

2. estimate; answers will vary.

3. Possible answers: Its museum and library were the best in the world. Great minds came there to study. The first dictionaries and encyclopedias were written there. Many things were invented there, such as the first musical instrument with a keyboard, and a system of punctuation and grammar.

Tyree's Song   p. 68

1. Possible answers: Tyree will play more concerts with Amadeus. He will try to play the music for his father.

2. Answers will vary.

3. Possible answers: Songs evolve and change as they are played. No song is played the same way twice. The best musicians are skilled at finding new and original patterns.

Cutters, Carvers, and the Cathedral   p. 69

1. Answers will vary.

2. Answers will vary.

3. Possible answers: Some wanted to learn a craft. Some wanted to be part of a huge creation like the cathedral. Some had worked on cathedrals in Europe. They enjoyed working with stone.

© Scott Foresman 6

Before Reading

For an overview of the content and skills within the *Collection for Readers*, see pages 36–37 of this handbook.

Preview and Predict Turn to the title page of the selection. Read the title and question aloud. Then ask students to preview the illustrations. Model using the text, pictures, and question to predict what the story will be about. Then ask students to make their predictions.

Set Purposes Ask students to think about what they might like to learn about the characters or events illustrated in the pictures. Students can use the question on the title page, or write their own question, to set a purpose for reading.

Vocabulary Point out vocabulary words that might be important to understanding the story. (See lists on pp. 86–93 of this handbook.) Whenever possible, use the pictures to help students understand meanings of words. You may want to have students generate a list of words they don't know. Talk with students about the words to help them make connections between vocabulary and story concepts and what students already know. If you want to use additional vocabulary strategies with students, see page 13 of this handbook for ideas.

During Reading

Story Structure Remind students that fiction has a beginning, a middle, and an end. The story, or plot, centers on a problem, or conflict, that is resolved by the end of the story. Students can use story structure to make sense of, or understand, the story.

Characters Work with students to identify the main character(s). Have students look for clues about the characters based on what they say, what they do, and what others say about them. Encourage them to refer to pictures for clues.

Setting Help students look for information about the setting—where and when the story takes place. What words does the author use to reveal the setting? Help students find details in the pictures that correspond to the words. Ask students to think about how much time passes in the story.

Plot Tell students to look for the problem in the story. How is the problem solved? Encourage students to think about what is the most important part of the story.

Theme As students read, they should think "What is this story really about?"

© Scott Foresman 6

Summarize Information Help students synthesize information and make inferences about the text. You might ask:

- What are the important events in this part of the story?
- What is the author trying to tell you about the character(s)?
- What is this part of the story all about?
- What new things happened in this part of the story?

Locate and Classify Details Ask questions that prompt students to locate and classify details. Sample questions might be:

- What details can you find to support your thinking?
- Where in the story does it say that?
- What part of the story made you think that?

Critical Thinking Help students analyze the text. Ask questions like:

- Why do you think the author wrote this story?
- What is the problem in the story?
- How do the characters change?
- Is the problem resolved in a believable way?

Reread Have students reread the selection as necessary to build fluency and understanding.

Use the Take-Home Readers The Take-Home version of the *Collection for Readers* can be used for rereading or activities such as coloring the pictures, and underlining key vocabulary.

After Reading

Discuss Talk with students about the predictions they made and the purpose they set for reading. Make connections to the topic or the unit theme of the selection.

Skill Practice Use Questions 1 and 2 in Looking Back to help students practice skills. See page 37 for an explanation of how Question 1 helps students routinely practice identifying the text or story structure and how Question 2 helps students practice five critical comprehension skills.

Critical Thinking Think About It or Talk About It, Question 3, asks students to think and talk critically about the story. Students relate the selection to their own lives or discuss their opinions about characters, plot, or theme with a partner. Sometimes students are asked to reflect about their own learning.

Before Reading

For an overview of the content and skills within the *Collection for Readers,* see pages 36-37 of this handbook.

Preview and Predict Read the story title aloud. Then ask students to preview the photographs, diagrams, and illustrations. Model using the text and pictures to predict what the selection will be about. Then ask students to make their predictions.

Set Purposes Ask students to think about what they already know about the topic. Remind students that what they already know about the topic will help them as they read. Then ask them what they would like to find out when they read the selection. You may want to have students use a K-W-L Chart or other graphic organizer. (See pp. 22–33 of this handbook.) Students can use the question on the title page, or write their own question, to set a purpose for reading.

Vocabulary Point out vocabulary words that might be important to understanding the selection. (See lists on pp. 86–93 of this handbook.) Whenever possible, use pictures and diagrams to help students understand meanings of words. You may want to have students generate a list of words they don't know. Talk with students about the words to help them make connections between vocabulary and selection concepts and what students already know about a topic. If you want to use additional vocabulary strategies with students, see page 13 of this handbook for suggestions.

During Reading

Text Structure Remind students that nonfiction selections provide information or explain something. Text structure refers to the way information is organized in a text. Students need to know how text is organized in order to find information. Show students how the author has organized information using titles, headings, captions, labels, questions, and other print features or graphic aids. Help students connect information in the text with photographs, diagrams, or illustrations.

Key Words Direct students to look for key words that signal the way the text is organized. Provide students with examples of key words to look for as they read.

Time Order: *first, next, before, after, last, later*

Cause and Effect: *because, since, as a result, due to, for this reason*

Compare and Contrast: *either, but, while, although, unlike*

© Scott Foresman 6

Summarize Information Help students synthesize information and make inferences about the text. You might ask:

- What is the most important idea?

- What is the author trying to say?

- What is this part of the selection all about?

- What new things have you learned?

Locate and Classify Details Ask questions that prompt students to locate and classify details. Sample questions might be:

- What details can you find to support your thinking?

- Where in the selection does it say that?

- What are some of the important ideas?

Critical Thinking Help students analyze the text. Ask questions like:

- Why do you think the author wrote this selection?

- How is this like other selections you have read?

- What did the author do to make you interested in the topic?

- What questions do you still have about the topic?

Reread Have students reread the selection as necessary to build fluency and understanding.

See also **Use the Take-Home Readers,** page 77.

After Reading

Discuss Talk with students about the predictions they made and the purpose they set for reading. Make connections to the topic or the unit theme of the selection.

Skill Practice Use Questions 1 and 2 in Looking Back to help students practice skills. See page 37 for an explanantion of how Question 1 helps students routinely practice identifying the text or story structure and how Question 2 helps students practice five critical comprehension skills.

Critical Thinking Think About It or Talk About It, Question 3, asks students to think and talk critically about the selection. This question leads students to think critically about the selection by relating it to their own lives or by discussing their opinions about people, events, or ideas with a partner. Some are metacognitive questions that help students reflect about their own learning.

Collection for Readers Answer Key

Cassey at Camp

1. **This story is about:** a girl who feels clumsy and has trouble fitting in at camp; **This story takes place:** at camp; **The main events are:** Cassey is embarrassed because she dropped the ball during a baseball game. Annie makes her feel bad for the mistake. The next day, sailing lessons begin. Cassey is excited about sailing. She listens carefully to the instructor. Annie and Cassey are partners. The girls do not speak much as they practice. Cassey is surprised when she is chosen by the instructor to sail in a race; **The story ends when:** Cassey wins the race for her cabin and is congratulated by her cabin mates and Annie.

2. Possible answers: Cassey plays baseball first. Cassey drops the ball.

3. Answers will vary. Students might say a good sport does not get angry when he or she loses a game or when somebody makes a mistake.

The Right Man for the Job

1. Possible answers: Main idea—Jackie Robinson was the right man to break the color barrier in the Major Leagues; Details—Robinson was a great athlete. Robinson was a second lieutenant in the army and fought against injustice by opening the door for African American soldiers to become officers. Robinson had the strength to quietly endure anger and mistreatment.

2. Possible answers: Robinson was patient and did not strike back when some of his teammates and fans were hostile toward him. Robinson spoke out against injustice by protesting hotels that refused to let him stay with his teammates. He also protested teams that refused to hire African American players.

3. Encourage students to look back in the article for information to support their answers.

The Potter's Hands

1. Possible answers: Characters—Dan, Maria Alvarez, Mom, Dad; Problem—Dan is having trouble with his schoolwork and isn't sure what will help; Events—First, Dan is supposed to do his homework, but leaves his home after school to visit the Alvarez house and watch Maria Alvarez make pottery in her studio. Dan goes to the studio every day after school. Mrs. Alvarez shows him how to shape pots in the traditional way. Dan tells Mrs. Alvarez about his trouble with schoolwork. She tells him about how her ancestors made sure that the young learned what they needed to get along in the world; Solution—By making pottery, Dan is happier. He talks about his schoolwork more with his parents and they help him with his homework.

2. Possible answers: Dan is happier and tries harder at his schoolwork.

3. Answers will vary.

Japanese Americans

1. Possible answers: Main idea—Japanese American children in the 1930s often felt as if they never completely belonged to the U.S. or Japan; Details—Japanese American children grew up knowing two different cultures and two different ways of life. Japanese American children wanted to be accepted at school but were often treated like foreigners. They had two names—a Japanese name used at home and an American name used at school.

2. Possible answers: Japanese American children felt like two people. They had American experiences, but they were Japanese because of their looks. They practiced Japanese customs and beliefs, but they lived in America.

3. Answers will vary.

Starting Over

1. Possible answers: Characters—Jordan, Matt, Cora, Tom; Problem—Matt and Jordan have a hard time getting along because of their differences; Events—First, Jordan and Matt's father loses his job in Mobile. Their family has to move to Vinton, Virginia. Jordan and Matt start a new school. While getting ready for school, the two argue. Then the two argue about a lunch time incident at school. Cora stops their arguing and tells them that brothers should stick together. Next, at supper Jordan and Matt tell their parents that they feel like outsiders at school. Their Dad says to find common ground with the kids at school. Mom tells them to be themselves. Last, after supper Matt helps Jordan with his homework. Matt tells Jordan he wishes he could talk to people the way Jordan does. Jordan tells Matt he wishes he was smart like Matt; Solution—Jordan and Matt learn to appreciate their differences and to get along.

2. Possible answers: Matt is tall and thin, he is a good student, and plans to be a doctor. Jordan is short with a stocky build, he is the class clown, and he doesn't think about the future.

Collection for Readers Answer Key

3. Answers will vary.

Something to Crow About

1. Possible answers: Main idea—Crows have attributes that make them very interesting; Details—Crows are very clever. Unlike most other birds, crows do not chase away their offspring and the young remain at home for years. Crows have over 23 patterns of caws and are good communicators.

2. Possible answers: Most leave their parents. Some stay and help their parents.

3. Answers will vary, but students should support their answers with information from the article or their own experience.

Survival Skills

1. Possible Answers: Cause—When you're lost, stay where you are; Effect—Others will miss you and start to search for you; Cause—When you hike, take water with you; Effect—Your mind and body will function better.

2. Possible answers: I would use garbage bags to provide warmth or shade. I would sit under low branches of a tree or scoop a hole in the ground to find shade when it is hot. I would stay off the bare ground and gather leaves and branches to sit on when it is cold. I would build a fire using tinder, kindling, and fuel to keep warm.

3. Students may say that previewing the pictures and headings helped them understand the article and got them interested in reading it.

Thirsty Land

1. Possible answers: Cause—Drought; Effect—Crops, grasses, and trees dry up; Cause—Drought; Effect—Lakes, rivers, and streams shrink.

2. Possible answers: Land that is fertile becomes a desert. Animal habitats such as wetlands may be lost. Endangered species may not survive.

3. Answers will vary. Students should support their responses with information about their own experiences.

Save the Sea Turtle

1. Possible answers: Main idea—Many dangers threaten the survival of the sea turtle; Details—Beaches with buildings and lights confuse some hatchlings who need darkness to reach the sea. Polluted beaches can keep a turtle from crawling up the beach to nest. Turtles sometime die from eating plastic objects such as bags that they mistake for jellyfish.

2. Possible answers: Hatchlings are sometimes eaten by birds or fish before making it to deeper waters. Beaches with lights confuse hatchlings who follow the light, thinking it is the horizon out at sea.

3. Answers will vary. Students may say that it might be difficult to stop other animals from eating the sea turtles.

Oil Spills: Slick and Deadly

1. Possible answers: Main idea—People use different methods to clean up oil spills to prevent destruction to wildlife and the ecosystem; Details—A boom sets up a floating barrier and keeps the oil from spreading. Chemicals such as disperants or gelling agents can be used to break up oil into droplets. People can rake, wipe, or wash off the oil.

2. Possible answers: Some equipment doesn't work well in certain weather conditions so alternative tools are needed to help clean up oil spills.

3. Answers will vary. Students may say that they do not litter and could recycle garbage.

The Story of Elizabeth Blackwell

1. Possible answers: Problem—Elizabeth Blackwell faced many obstacles as a woman doctor; Solution—Elizabeth Blackwell overcame these obstacles by working hard in medical school and graduating first in her class, opening her own medical practice, and helping to found the New York Infirmary for Women and Children, the United States Sanitary Commission, the Women's Medical College in New York, and the London School of Medicine for Women.

2. Possible answers: Society did not believe that women were as capable as men. Society did not think women should be doctors.

3. Answers will vary. Students should support their answers with information from the article.

The Lot

1. Possible answers: Characters—Luis, Jorge, Nana, Mom, Mr. Marquez, Mr. and Mrs.

© Scott Foresman 6

Ramirez, Mrs. Stokely, Ron Herrera; Problem—Luis is angry about a dangerous, vacant lot filled with trash; Events—First, Luis and his friends play soccer in the street. Then Nana hurts her foot on a piece of metal in the vacant lot. Next, Luis talks to his friends about cleaning the trash in the lot. They all agree to help on Saturday, except Jorge. Mr. and Mrs. Ramirez help the boys. The next Saturday, Jorge helps. After a few weeks, the lot is clean. Mrs. Stokely brings grass seeds to plant. Last, everybody decides the lot would make a great park. They talk to the city councilman and come up with a plan for the park. The neighborhood would raise money for the park and the city would match the money raised; Solution—Luis helped make a good change in his neighborhood by getting others to work together to clean a vacant lot.

2. Possible answers: Jorge doesn't think it is his job to clean up the lot and doesn't help. Luis is determined to clean the lot and gets others to help. Jorge and Luis both play soccer. Like Luis, Jorge ends up helping clean the lot.

3. Students may say that the pictures help them understand the order in which events are happening in the story.

Super Women of Sports

1. Possible answers: Main idea—Super women athletes of the past influenced future super women athletes; Details—By winning a gold medal in the 1932 Olympics, Babe Zaharias helped change the attitude that women should not be athletes. Wilma Rudolph became the first American woman to win three gold medals in one Olympics and was called the fastest woman in the world. Jackie Joyner-Kersee was Wilma Rudolph's friend and she was influenced by her great feats.

2. Possible answers: Wilma made her leg strong with exercise and no longer needed a leg brace. Wilma's hard work turned her into a great athlete who accomplished many feats.

3. Encourage students to look back in the article for information to support their ideas.

Last Man Up in Mudville

1. Possible answers: Characters—Cooney, Burrows, Flynn, Blake, Casey, the umpire, the crowd; Problem—The Mudville team is losing the game and the crowd thinks Casey could

help win the game; Events—First, the score is four to two against the team in the bottom of the ninth. Cooney and Burrows both get a hit but get tagged out at first base. Flynn and Blake hit next. Flynn hits a single. Blake hits a double, sending Flynn to third base. Then Casey steps into the box. Casey watches the first pitch whiz by. The umpire shouts "Strike!" Next, the crowd gets angry at the umpire. Casey ignores the next pitch and the umpire says "Strike two!" Casey swings at the next pitch and strikes out; Ending—Even Casey couldn't win the game for Mudville.

2. Possible answers: Mudville is at bat, but they are losing four to two. Cooney and Burrows both get a hit, but get tagged out at first. Flynn hits a single and Blake hits a double.

3. Encourage students to look back in the story for clues to support their ideas.

Planets in a Row

1. Possible answers: Main idea—How to plan a model of the solar system; Details—Gather information about the planets before you build the model. Determine whether or not you can build the model to scale. Make your model interesting.

2. Possible answers: The **inner part** has four planets that are close to the sun, are heavy and slow moving, and are made mostly of rock and metal. The **outer part** has five planets that are light for their size and are made mostly of hydrogen and helium.

3. Students may say that looking at diagrams, tables, and captions helped them to understand what the article was about.

Why the Wild Flowers Grow

1. **This story is about:** a girl who learns why wild flowers grow; **This story takes place:** at the girl's grandmother's house and in a garden; **The main events are:** A little girl picks flowers for her aunt. The aunt tells the girl she hurt the flowers. Grandmother tells the girl a story about why the Choctaw do not pick flowers. She tells her about how Bright Eyes and her sisters came down from the sky to Earth to make people happy. On their way to Earth, the sisters learned how to weave from Uncta. Once on earth, they taught the Choctaw how to weave rugs and blankets to protect themselves from the cold. Bright Eyes and her sisters prayed to the Great Spirit to

Collection for Readers Answer Key

protect the people. As the prayers got to the Great Spirit, he changed them into flowers and dropped seeds upon the Earth. Bright Eyes and her sisters planted the seeds. The people never picked the flowers because they were a token from the Great Spirit; **The story ends when:** the girl tells her grandmother that she understands the importance of the flowers and would not pick them.

2. Possible answer: Bright Eyes and her sisters go to Mount Joy and meet the great spider, Uncta.

3. Answers will vary.

The Lady with the Lamp

1. Possible answers: Main idea—France and the United States worked together to build a statue that represented liberty; Details—The French built the statue and the Americans built the pedestal on which it stands. The French held a lottery and sold clay models of the statue to raise enough money for its completion. Joseph Pulitzer urged Americans to donate money to help build the statue's pedestal, saying it was "a gift of the whole people of France to the whole people of America."

2. Answers will vary.

3. Answers will vary. Students may say the American Flag is a symbol of freedom and that they see it at school.

Something From Nothing

1. Possible answers: Topic—Folk artists make something out of nothing; Alike—Folk artists make art out of common materials. They usually are not trained to be artists; Different—Some of these folk artists used bottles to make art while others used toothpicks; Conclusion—Folk artists aren't trained to be artists but can make art out of common materials.

2. Possible answer: A good folk artist needs to be able to look at everyday objects differently and make something new out of them.

3. Answers will vary.

The Wonder of Ancient Egypt

1. Possible answers: Main idea—The builders of the Great Pyramid had remarkable skill and knowledge; Details—The builders had no heavy machinery, yet they were able to move blocks weighing 2 to 70 tons each; Workers were able to cut the outer stones perfectly

straight. The Pyramid is built mathematically exact.

2. Possible answers: People believe it took 20,000 people working 20 years to build the Great Pyramid. The Pyramid was built using 2,300,000 limestone and granite blocks that weighed 2.5 to 50 tons each.

3. Encourage students to look back in the article for information to support their ideas.

We Are All One

1. Possible answers: Characters—the old peddler, the peddler's wife, the rich man, the ants, the caterpillar, the gatekeeper; Problem—The rich man has an eye disease and said he would reward anyone who can find a cure; Events—First, the rich man offers the reward to anyone who can cure his disease. The peddler goes to look for a leaf buried in the forest that has powers to heal the eyes. Along the way, he helps some ants. Then he looks for a place to sleep and finds a caterpillar running from a bird. The bird wants to eat the caterpillar. The peddler shoes the bird away. Next, he falls asleep and hears a voice telling him where to find the leaf. He goes to the spot where the voice said he would find the leaf. But his eyes are too weak and he cannot see. Some ants help find the bead. Last, the peddler gives the leaf to the rich man. The man is cured; Solution—By helping others the peddler is helped in the end.

2. Possible answers: The old peddler helps save the ants' nest. He saves the caterpillar from being eaten by a bird.

3. Answers will vary.

Life at the Pole

1. Possible answers: Main idea—Life survives at the North Pole because the animals that live there are adapted to cold weather. Details—The Arctic fox has the warmest fur of any mammal. Seals have sleek furry bodies and a layer of blubber to insulate them. The skin beneath a polar bear's fur is black and allows it to absorb heat from the sun.

2. Possible answers: Temperatures can be -70°F or less. Snow never melts. All you see is ice and snow.

3. Students may say that previewing the map and photographs helped them to understand where the North Pole is and what animals the article features.

Collection for Readers Answer Key

A Trip to Remember

1. Possible answers: Topic—Traveling from Mexico City to California through a rain forest; Alike—The city is bustling with activity. The government is there, and a variety of foods is available. The Aztec and Mayan civilizations were complex as well. Religion in Mexico is a combination of Spanish and native beliefs. The culture and people are also a blend of Spanish and native roots; Different—The city has comfortable houses. Villages in the country have no hotels and only a few shelters in which travelers can stay. The city is full of people and buildings. The rain forest is filled with plants, animals, and insects, some of which are poisonous; Conclusion—While going from Mexico City to California through a rain forest, a traveler will see a variety of people, places, and animals.

2. Possible answers: In 1876, Mexico City was a large, bustling city. The government was located there. Many foods were available. People shopped in a large outdoor market. There were also many churches in the city. In the outlying countryside, there were small stone buildings and shelters. No hotels were available there.

3. Answers will vary.

Mars and Martians

1. Possible answers: Cause—Spacecraft took pictures of Mars' surface to give us our first view of the planet; Effect—In the 1960s, scientists learned more information about Mars. They learned Mars did not support life but did have craters, the largest volcano ever seen, and a canyon larger than the U.S. is wide; Cause—A meteorite was found in Antarctica that scientists think came from Mars; Effect—In 1996, the discovery renewed interest in Mars.

2. Answers will vary. Students may say yes because NASA is making plans to send astronauts to Mars to live as colonists and study the planet.

3. Encourage students to look back in the article for information to support their ideas.

Nightmare on Dessert Island

1. Possible answers: Characters—Sam, Beezle, Granny; Problem—Sam wants to eat only junk food; Events—First, Sam reads a note from her mom saying she found cupcakes hidden in Sam's closet. Sam finds a letter saying she has won a trip to a Dessert Island. She takes a plane to the island. Sam is greeted by Beezle, a troll. Then Beezle takes Sam to her hotel. Beezle brings her all the desserts she wants. Next, Sam starts to lose her energy. She wakes up and feels terrible. She asks Beezle for an egg to eat. Beezle says that Sam's contract doesn't allow her to ask for such food. Next, Sam discovers that she is to work one month for every day she is a guest at the island. Sam tries to escape down a river. She meets Granny. Last, Granny helps Sam escape from the trolls chasing her. Sam ends up in her kitchen. It is all a dream; Solution—Sam learns that eating only junk food may not be very good for her.

2. Possible answers: It stops being fun when she feels her clothes getting tight. Then she wants good food but finds out she can't have any.

3. Encourage students to look back in the story for details to support their ideas.

The Real Cowboy

1. Possible answers: Main idea—The images of cowboys portrayed in the movies weren't how cowboys really were; Details—A cowboy's life was harder than what is presented in the movies. Most cowboys obeyed the laws and were not violent like how movies portray them. Cowboys did not lead the adventurous lives that cowboy characters do in movies.

2. Possible answers: Between 1866 and 1886 many Americans moved West to become cattle ranchers and they needed cowboys. Ranchers began using barbed wire in 1890 to keep their cattle from roaming the open ranch.

3. Encourage students to look back in the article for information to support their ideas.

When Grandma Came to Stay

1. Possible answers: Characters—Susan, Sheri, Shane, Mom, Dan, Grandma Bernice; Problem—Susan is upset when she has to give up her room for her Grandma Bernice; Events—First, Susan is upset that she has to give up her room for Grandma Bernice. Susan tries to avoid greeting Grandma Bernice when she arrives. Then during the week, Susan and her family enjoy spending time with Grandma Bernice. Next, Sheri makes a mess on Susan's

notebook and comforter. Susan runs to tell her mother. When Grandma Bernice tries to calm Susan down, Susan says something hurtful. Last, Susan goes to apologize to Grandma Bernice. Grandma Bernice shows Susan some hair ornaments that once belonged to her Grandma Susan. She tells Susan that she once had to share a room with her Grandmother. She said she didn't want to share, but she ended up having fun with her Grandmother. Grandma Bernice gives Susan her grandmother's hair ornaments; Solution— Susan realizes that living with her Grandmother could be something she could look forward to doing.

2. Possible answers: Susan will probably get along well with her grandmother and the rest of her family.

3. Encourage students to look back in the story for details to support their ideas.

Making a Light in the Darkness

1. Possible answers: Problem—Louis Braille wanted to improve the method blind people used for reading; Solutions—Louis learned about "night writing" which is a tactile code of dots and dashes used by soilders. He studied the code and tried to make it less cumbersome. Then he made it simpler by developing a system that used six raised dots to represent the alphabet code so the blind could read faster and easier.

2. Answer: Louis Braille's first book was not accepted right away because people who were not blind couldn't understand how useful Braille could be. Blind people loved Braille because they could read more quickly.

3. Students may say that the graphic organizer helped them to understand what the problem was in the article and how it was solved.

Demetrius of Alexandria

1. Possible answers: Characters—Demetrius, Pappus; Setting—the city streets, the great library of Alexandria; Events—Demetrius goes to the library every day and plays his lyre while Pappus works. He also brings food to Pappus and asks him many questions. Demetrius's father and grandfather want Demetrius to be a scholar. One day Demetrius overhears two scholars talking about astronomy. He asks Pappus questions about the stars. Demetrius decides he wants to become a scholar and learn more about astronomy.

2. Answers will vary. Encourage students to use details from the story and from their own lives to respond to the question.

3. Answers will vary.

The Aliens

1. **This story is about:** Julie, Sandy, Nate, Amy, Anthony, and Louis exploring another planet; **This story takes place:** in the crew's ship and on another planet; **The main events are:** The crew lands on a planet. They meet four creatures. The crew uses a language translator to understand what the creatures are saying. The creatures take the crew to a beautiful building. After the crew eats dinner, a computer rises from the table. The creatures ask Sandy to make a model of Earth homes. **The story ends when:** the crew returns to their ship. They say they didn't feel like aliens because the creatures were so friendly to them.

2. Possible answers: The crew and the creatures became friends during the meal. Julie declared their mission a success at the very end.

3. Students may say that the story map helped them understand how the events in the story happened and what the story was about.

From Blueprints to Buildings

1. Possible answers: Main idea—An architect plans and designs buildings and other structures for a living; Details—Architects work with clients to determine what the building will be used for and how much it will cost. Architects use computer programs to create the blueprints builders use to build the structure. Architects use skills such as the ability to analyze things, to problem solve, and to picture how a structure will look.

2. Possible answers: Some architects work on projects from start to finish. Other architects specialize in just one part of their profession while others specialize in restoring older buildings.

3. Encourage students to look back in the article for information to support their ideas.

Unit 1 Selection 1

Cassey at Camp

Comprehension Skill: Sequence

Vocabulary for Concept Development
capsized
lessons
sailboat
tiller
excited
mast

High-Frequency Words
start
knew
could
right
remember
after

Unit 1 Selection 2

The Right Man for the Job

Comprehension Skill: Main Idea and Details

Vocabulary for Concept Development
athlete
endure
hostile
injustice
magnificent
segregated

High-Frequency Words
began
would
knew
more
of
some

Unit 1 Selection 3

The Potter's Hands

Comprehension Skill: Cause and Effect

Vocabulary for Concept Development
adobe
pottery
studio
ancestors
traditional
horno

High-Frequency Words
father
mother
ground
work
house
help

Unit 1 Selection 4

Japanese Americans

Comprehension Skill: Drawing Conclusions

Vocabulary for Concept Development
favorite
celebrate
traditional
feast
homeland
kimono
foreigner

High-Frequency Words
new
old
different
not
food
would

Unit 1 Selection 5

Starting Over

Comprehension Skill: Compare and Contrast

Vocabulary for Concept Development
cope
tactful
objective
empathy
obvious
indignantly

High-Frequency Words
could
down
good
he
their
how

Unit 2 Selection 1

Something to Crow About

Comprehension Skill: Sequence

Vocabulary for Concept Development
clever
brood
communicate
predator
roost
territory
attributes

High-Frequency Words
eat
family
know
good
they
when

Unit 2 Selection 2

Survival Skills

Comprehension Skill: Compare and Contrast

Vocabulary for Concept Development
wilderness
shelter
tinder
kindling
flammable
ignite

High-Frequency Words
because
cold
for
make
with
your

Unit 2 Selection 3

Thirsty Land

Comprehension Skill: Cause and Effect

Vocabulary for Concept Development
drought
climate
desert
migrate
soil

High-Frequency Words
animals
your
Earth
is
many
see

Unit 2 Selection 4

Save the Sea Turtle

Comprehension Skill: Main Idea and Details

Vocabulary for Concept Development
jellyfish
flippers
hatchling
millions
protect
predators

High-Frequency Words
across
can
have
long
to
until

Unit 2 Selection 5

Oil Spills: Slick and Deadly

Comprehension Skill: Drawing Conclusions

Vocabulary for Concept Development
contaminated
ecosystem
equipment
insulate
marine
slick
dispersants

High-Frequency Words
clean
off
or
so
animals
there

Unit 3 Selection 1

The Story of Elizabeth Blackwell

Comprehension Skill: Drawing Conclusions

Vocabulary for Concept Development
infection
capable
rejection
surgeon
practice
inspired

High-Frequency Words
saw
great
finally
grow
become

Unit 3 Selection 2

The Lot

Comprehension Skill: Compare and Contrast

Vocabulary for Concept Development
attitude
laborers
debris
neighborhood
involved
agreed

High-Frequency Words
by
but
few
friends
people
play

Unit 3 Selection 3

Super Women of Sports

Comprehension Skill: Cause and Effect

Vocabulary for Concept Development
ability
obstacle
attitude
natural
professional
athlete

High-Frequency Words
become
as
have
her
great
could

Unit 3 Selection 4

Last Man Up in Mudville

Comprehension Skill: Sequence

Vocabulary for Concept Development
bearing
defiance
grandeur
haughty
multitude
tumult
writhed

High-Frequency Words
and
at
but
it
not
out

Unit 3 Selection 5

Planets in a Row

Comprehension Skill: Main Idea and Details

Vocabulary for Concept Development
orbit
planet
asteroid
solar system
diameter
scale
model

High-Frequency Words
make
that
big
you
how
they

Unit 4 Selection 1

Why the Wild Flowers Grow

Comprehension Skill: Sequence

Vocabulary for Concept Development
ancestors
scent
stalks
forest
protect
delighted
blossoms

High-Frequency Words
earth
her
story
beautiful
most
why

Unit 4 Selection 2

The Lady with the Lamp

Comprehension Skill: Compare and Contrast

Vocabulary for Concept Development
copper
donations
gigantic
liberty
pedestal
symbol

High-Frequency Words
at
was
place
she
people
together

Unit 4 Selection 3

Something from Nothing

Comprehension Skill: Drawing Conclusions

Vocabulary for Concept Development
folk
artist
materials
recycled
common
drawings

High-Frequency Words
something
did
from
nothing
pictures
used

Unit 4 Selection 4

The Wonder of Ancient Egypt

Comprehension Skill: Main Idea and Details

Vocabulary for Concept Development
pharaoh
tomb
massive
exactly
remarkable
marvel
structure

High-Frequency Words
probably
able
would
used
great
people

Unit 4 Selection 5

We Are All One

Comprehension Skill: Cause and Effect

Vocabulary for Concept Development
treasure
distressed
recovery
impatience
deserted
realized
shelter

High-Frequency Words
all
one
he
old
enough
went

Unit 5 Selection 1

Life at the Pole

Comprehension Skill: Main Idea and Details

Vocabulary for Concept Development
Arctic
blubber
enemy
adapt
polar
tundra
horizon

High-Frequency Words
has
cold
move
open
them
under

Unit 5 Selection 2

A Trip to Remember

Comprehension Skill: Compare and Contrast

Vocabulary for Concept Development
adventure
journey
comfortable
shelter
dangerous

High-Frequency Words
and
carry
high
many
are
road

Unit 5 Selection 3

Mars and Martians

Comprehension Skill: Drawing Conclusions

Vocabulary for Concept Development
technology
radiation
organisms
conditions
bacteria
experiments

High-Frequency Words
about
live
time
once
what
will

Unit 5 Selection 4

Nightmare on Dessert Island

Comprehension Skill: Sequence

Vocabulary for Concept Development
envelope
expectations
afternoon
travelers
exclaimed

High-Frequency Words
be
bring
food
how
taste
we

Unit 5 Selection 5

The Real Cowboy

Comprehension Skill: Cause and Effect

Vocabulary for Concept Development
cattles
chuckwagon
cowboys
ranchers
range
roundup
trail drive

High-Frequency Words
what
keep
picture
different
open
work

Unit 6 Selection 1

When Grandma Came to Stay

Comprehension Skill: Drawing Conclusions

Vocabulary for Concept Development
anticipation
comforter
ornaments
privacy
wheelchair

High-Frequency Words
would
young
pretty
room
she
mother

Unit 6 Selection 2

Making a Light in the Darkness

Comprehension Skill: Cause and Effect

Vocabulary for Concept Development
accepted
institute
tactile
embossed
cumbersome
tuberculosis

High-Frequency Words
about
heard
new
read
school
were

Unit 6 Selection 3

Demetrius of Alexandria

Comprehension Skill: Compare and Contrast

Vocabulary for Concept Development
scholar
cistern
constellations
dissected
lyre
promenade
curious

High-Frequency Words
animals
boy
father
great
thought
work

© Scott Foresman 6

Unit 6 Selection 4

The Aliens

Comprehension Skill: Sequence

Vocabulary for Concept Development
acoustics
alien
maneuvered
retracted
suction
tolerable
variations

High-Frequency Words
blue
down
we
them
red
yellow

Unit 6 Selection 5

From Blueprints to Building

Comprehension Skill: Main Idea and Details

Vocabulary for Concept Development
architect
blueprint(s)
specialize
construction
restore
structures

High-Frequency Words
all
do
must
show
start
think

Collection for Readers
Grades 3-6

Comprehension Skill	Grade 3	Grade 4	Grade 5	Grade 6
Cause and Effect	*Unit 1* Up All Night *Unit 2* Tip of the Iceberg *Unit 3* Pretend You're Not Afraid *Unit 4* Dragons for Breakfast *Unit 5* Booker T. Washington *Unit 6* The Mail Must Go Through	*Unit 1* Snow on the Prairie *Unit 2* Life on the Prairie *Unit 3* A Dangerous Storm *Unit 4* How Earth Learned to Sing *Unit 5* American Peddlers *Unit 6* A Rockin' Good Time	*Unit 1* The Negro Leagues *Unit 2* Hurricane! *Unit 3* The First Day *Unit 4* Pizza with Grandma *Unit 5* A Famous Messenger *Unit 6* The Garden Wall	*Unit 1* The Potter's Hands *Unit 2* Thirsty Land *Unit 3* Super Women of Sports *Unit 4* We Are All One *Unit 5* The Real Cowboy *Unit 6* Making a Light in the Darkness
Compare and Contrast	*Unit 1* The City Mouse and the Country Mouse *Unit 2* Birds of the Water *Unit 3* The Rabbit and the Turtle *Unit 4* The Raja's Contest *Unit 5* Hard Times on the Farm *Unit 6* A View from Space	*Unit 1* Just Like Home *Unit 2* City Gardens *Unit 3* The Greatest Lumberjack Ever *Unit 4* The Three Little Pigs and the Big Bad Wolf *Unit 5* Early Cars *Unit 6* American Inventions	*Unit 1* My Friend Marissa *Unit 2* Playful Pals *Unit 3* The Cat That Was Part Dog *Unit 4* Dinner with the Tanakas *Unit 5* The Fight to Vote *Unit 6* Break a Leg!	*Unit 1* Starting Over *Unit 2* Survival Skills *Unit 3* The Lot *Unit 4* The Lady with the Lamp *Unit 5* A Trip to Remember *Unit 6* Demetrius of Alexandria
Drawing Conclusions	*Unit 1* The Rodeo *Unit 2* Watch Out for Twisters *Unit 3* Making Pictures for a Book *Unit 4* The Tale of Retaw Yob *Unit 5* Charles Lindbergh, Making History *Unit 6* Brownies for Breakfast	*Unit 1* Come to a Fiesta! *Unit 2* A Friendly, Furry Pet *Unit 3* Tiger in the Moonlight *Unit 4* Korea Today *Unit 5* North to the Pole *Unit 6* The Boy Who Dreamed	*Unit 1* Little Italy *Unit 2* Wetlands *Unit 3* The Iron Horse *Unit 4* Born to Run *Unit 5* Sugihara's Visas *Unit 6* Real Art	*Unit 1* Japanese Americans *Unit 2* Oil Spills: Slick and Deadly *Unit 3* The Story of Elizabeth Blackwell *Unit 4* Something from Nothing *Unit 5* Mars and Martians *Unit 6* When Grandma Came to Stay

© Scott Foresman 6

Comprehension Skill	Grade 3	Grade 4	Grade 5	Grade 6
Main Idea and Details	*Unit 1* Girls Just Want to Play Hoops *Unit 2* Plant Traps! *Unit 3* Some Special Dogs *Unit 4* Thunderstorms *Unit 5* Tokyo Today *Unit 6* Fiesta Fun	*Unit 1* New Homes for Orphans *Unit 2* Monsters, Dragons, and Other Reptiles *Unit 3* Heroes of the Pampas *Unit 4* Lucky Lou *Unit 5* Where Are We? *Unit 6* Native American Art	*Unit 1* The First Orphan Train *Unit 2* Make the World a Better Place *Unit 3* Making Honey *Unit 4* Run Like the Wind *Unit 5* A Woman Named Harriet *Unit 6* Are You going to Eat That?	*Unit 1* The Right Man for the Job *Unit 2* Save the Sea Turtle *Unit 3* Planets in a Row *Unit 4* The Wonder of Ancient Egypt *Unit 5* Life at the Pole *Unit 6* From Blueprints to Buildings
Sequence	*Unit 1* I Would Like to Visit a Fantastic Place *Unit 2* ROCK from TOCK *Unit 3* Good Game! *Unit 4* Stone Soup *Unit 5* Snowdance *Unit 6* Outside the Barn	*Unit 1* Chores Can Be Fun *Unit 2* City Cousin and Country Cousin *Unit 3* Timber! *Unit 4* I Was There *Unit 5* Sea Turtles *Unit 6* Gone from the Patio	*Unit 1* A Great Invention *Unit 2* The Ripe Red Apple Mystery *Unit 3* You Go, Girl! *Unit 4* The Sunrise Dance *Unit 5* A Trip to the Museum *Unit 6* The Weak Old Woman	*Unit 1* Cassey at Camp *Unit 2* Something to Crow About *Unit 3* Last Man Up in Mudville *Unit 4* Why the Wild Flowers Grow *Unit 5* Nightmare on Dessert Island *Unit 6* The Aliens

Leveled Readers 1–6

Comprehension Skill	Leveled Readers for Grade 1	Leveled Readers for Grade 2	Leveled Readers for Grade 3	Leveled Readers for Grade 4	Leveled Readers for Grade 5	Leveled Readers for Grade 6
Author's Purpose	5A, 5B, 16A, 16B	33A, 33B	63A, 63B, 84A, 84B	94A, 94B, 114A, 114B, 120A, 120B	124A, 124B, 140A, 140B	170A, 170B
Cause and Effect	2A, 2B, 6A, 6B, 22A, 22B, 24A, 24B	43A, 43B	64A, 64B, 78A, 78B	97A, 97B	124A, 124B	153A, 153B, 163A, 163B
Character	12A, 12B	32A, 32B, 44A, 44B, 52A, 52B	65A, 65B	95A, 95B	122A, 122B, 131A, 131B	155A, 155B, 175A, 175B
Compare and Contrast	7A, 7B, 20A, 20B, 27A, 27B	36A, 36B, 38A, 38B	79A, 79B	93A, 93B, 107A, 107B	136A, 136B	162A, 162B
Context Clues	1A, 1B, 11A, 11B	42A, 42B, 57A, 57B	68A, 68B	100A, 100B	139A, 139B, 144A, 144B	172A, 172B
Drawing Conclusions	8A, 8B, 30A, 30B	35A, 35B	62A, 62B	102A, 102B, 105A, 105B	130A, 130B	161A, 161B
Fact and Opinion		53A, 53B	69A, 69B, 82A, 82B	118A, 118B	128A, 128B	171A, 171B, 180A, 180B
Generalizing			75A, 75B	103A, 103B	123A, 123B	154A, 154B, 176A, 176B
Graphic Sources		39A, 39B, 54A, 54B	66A, 66B	113A, 113B	127A, 127B, 132A, 132B	178A, 178B
Main Idea and Supporting Details	9A, 9B, 15A, 15B, 23A, 23B	51A, 51B, 55A, 55B	70A, 70B	119A, 119B	137A, 137B	168A, 168B
Making Judgments		50A, 50B, 60A, 60B	81A, 81B	101A, 101B	149A, 149B	156A, 156B
Paraphrasing				106A, 106B	142A, 142B, 145A, 145B	179A, 179B
Plot	17A, 17B, 28A, 28B	49A, 49B, 58A, 58B	85A, 85B, 89A, 89B	110A, 110B, 112A, 112B	133A, 133B, 148A, 148B	167A, 167B
Predicting	3A, 3B, 19A, 19B	31A, 31B	80A, 80B, 83A, 83B	104A, 104B	138A, 138B	157A, 157B
Sequence	21A, 21B, 25A, 25B	40A, 40B	61A, 61B	92A, 92B	121A, 121B	151A, 151B
Setting	4A, 4B	34A, 34B	77A, 77B, 87A, 87B	91A, 91B	141A, 141B	158A, 158B
Steps in a Process		37A, 37B	71A, 71B, 86A, 86B	117A, 117B	126A, 126B, 147A, 147B	173A, 173B
Summarizing		41A, 41B, 45A, 45B	72A, 72B	109A, 109B, 111A, 111B	135A, 135B	164A, 164B, 174A, 174B
Text Structure			73A, 73B	98A, 98B, 108A, 108B, 115A, 115B	134A, 134B	169A, 169B
Theme	14A, 14B, 26A, 26B, 29A, 29B	47A, 47B, 59A, 59B	76A, 76B	99A, 99B	146A, 146B	165A, 165B
Visualizing			74A, 74B, 88A, 88B	96A, 96B, 116A, 116B	143A, 143B, 150A, 150B	159A, 159B

Each of the above Leveled Readers has its own instructional plan in the Leveled Reader Resource Guide.

© Scott Foresman 6